THE WHOLE-PERSON WORKPLACE

BUILDING BETTER WORKPLACES THROUGH WORK-LIFE, WELLNESS, AND EMPLOYEE SUPPORT

Scott Behson

AUTHORS PLACE
— PRESS —

Published by Authors Place Press
9885 Wyecliff Drive, Suite 200
Highlands Ranch, CO 80126
Authorsplace.com

Manufactured in the United States of America.

ISBN: 978-1-62865-815-6

CONTENTS

"NEVER TOOK THE ELEVATOR AGAIN"

"WE'RE OBSESSED WITH THE OTHER 4%"

"ARE WE GOING TO BUY 35,000 LAPTOPS?"

"BRINGING THEIR WHOLE SELVES TO WORK"

PRAISE FOR THE WHOLE-PERSON WORKPLACE

The Whole-Person Workplace is both timeless and timely. It's a practical guide for employers looking to establish a highly engaged culture that is built on a sustainable work/life balance. And it incorporates important insights on the rapidly expanding remote workforce. Highly recommended for CEOs, HR professionals, and any manager looking to attract, engage and retain first-rate talent.

—Dave Bolotsky, CEO of Uncommon Goods

Through years of trials and tribulations we were able to develop an environment that allowed our employees the ability to experience their own personal growth through better health, productivity, and work-life balance. Supporting employees during all the challenges in their lives is a crucial challenge for employers today, and *The Whole-Person Workplace* is a friendly, smart, practical guide for leaders and employers of all sizes.

—G. Brint Ryan, CEO of Ryan, LLC

Talk about timely... At the exact moment when, due to a global pandemic, nearly every organization is engaged in re-thinking the future of the workplace, Scott Behson has authored a book that offers a fresh way of thinking about employees and work. His approach calls on employers to embrace a new, whole-person approach to how they think about the needs of their people, both inside and outside of the workplace. *The Whole Person Workplace* offers ideas that will help employers right now as they attempt to envision the organizational culture that will attract top talent in the years to come.

—Brad Harrington, Executive Director and Research Professor,
Boston College Center for Work & Family

Behson's *The Whole-Person Workplace* is a timely, practical, idea-packed guide for addressing employer and employee needs in the new world of work.

—Scott Tannenbaum, President, The Group for Organizational Effectiveness and co-author of *Teams That Work*

Pre-pandemic, parents fought to make work-from-home accessible, today everyone is learning to live with what they wished for. The work-life conversation jumped ahead 10 years and Behson's book is the guide employers need for this new world. Stepping beyond the broken "accommodation" framework, Behson explores what it means to craft an agile and responsive workplace that sustains employees so it can achieve results.

—Kenneth Matos, Director of People Science at Culture Amp

As the founder of a fully remote team of more than 100 people at FlexJobs and Remote.co, I've long been committed to the idea that companies need to acknowledge and support The Whole Person in each of their team members. With Covid's long-lasting impacts on the workforce still to be determined, Scott's book provides critical insights to help leaders develop cultures and teams that embrace each person's whole self. It's not only good for people, it's also a healthy business practice that supports long-term success.

—Sara Sutton, Founder and CEO of Flexjobs

If you're like most managers, you've long wished you had a guidebook of best practices to help you navigate this brave new world of remote work. My advice? Read this book. Scott Behson is an expert at integrating work with life and has compiled a wealth of actionable advice in a friendly, accessible tone. *The Whole-Person Workplace* will help you discover new ways to support your employees in ways that reliably drive employee retention, engagement, and long-term performance. This book is a must-read for today's business leader and would make a smart addition to any MBA curriculum.

—Ron Friedman, Ph.D., author of
The Best Place to Work and *Decoding Greatness*

Scott Behson's Whole Person approach to work-life integration should be required reading as a way to foster a more lucid understanding around the economic and moral imperatives in building more adaptive and flexible work environments. Whether you're an HR leader or new to the workforce, Behson provides a commonsense approach that should guide policy and behavior through the Great Acceleration and beyond.

—Michael Rothman, Co-Founder and CEO at Fatherly

Scott's book brings forward the realization that the line between home and work of the last century, that became blurred in this century; via technology and the identification of "culture" as an important recruitment/retention initiative, has been erased with the pandemic. Readers of ***The Whole-Person Workplace*** will gain impactful insight into how to catch up to the importance of recognizing employees as "whole people."

—Anthony Oland, Global Chief People Officer at Boxed

Thanks to Scott Behson for this welcome addition to the literature on up-to-date, practical ways leaders at all levels can create positive change to better support employees in all aspects of their lives.

—Stew Friedman, award-winning Wharton professor
and bestselling author of *Total Leadership*

As pioneers in technology, we support employers across Federal, State and Local government lines, with the necessary tools to work and collaborate securely in any remote or mobile environment. Above all, we understand that enabling a workforce that is healthy in both body and mind is key to business continuity plans. Building a premier employee experience by supporting people in all areas of their lives is a crucial challenge for employers today, and *The Whole-Person Workplace* is a value-added, practical guide for employers of all sizes. Though we cannot predict the end to the COVID-19 crisis, nor the beginning of the next, the right kinds of supportive workforce measures can help mitigate the impacts. Many employers are struggling to adapt to a new post-Covid normal, and this book provides ideas and insights that will help them adjust to the future of work.

—Steve Nguyen, Vice President and
General Manager of Public Sector at Citrix

Dr. Behson's book offers an excellent, real-world resource for helping students contextualize the importance of effective human capital management, and provides a gold mine of actionable insights that any organization can implement and benefit from immediately.

—J. Bruce Tracey, Professor of Human Resources,
School of Hotel Administration at the SC Johnson College
of Business, Cornell University

DEDICATION

This book is dedicated to everyone who did their best through the Covid crisis, especially those who tried to make things better for others.

PREFACE – THE IMPORTANCE OF A WHOLE-PERSON APPROACH

FOR THIS BOOK, I interviewed over four dozen business leaders and other experts about their approaches to building Whole-Person Workplaces[1]. I started every interview by asking, "How important is it for employers to help employees address their work-life challenges, and what makes you say that?"

Before you dive into the book, I want to share some of my favorite direct quotes about how engaging employees as whole people results in business success and keeps you, as an employer, ahead of the game.

I've been here 28 years; I've seen it all. Considering where we came from and now that we've embraced supporting employees and working flexibly, I can see the huge difference in every key metric- productivity, engagement, satisfaction, turnover, productivity, client service, revenue. A huge win-win for everyone.

—Ginny Kissling, Global President and Chief Operating Officer, Ryan, LLC

It's a competitive advantage, especially in a tight labor market. Employee retention is gold, so I look at serving employees not as a simple expense but as an investment. If you genuinely care about employees, you engender loyalty and you create built-in recruiters who spread the work about working for you. Sometimes it's a real surprise for people, especially if they're used to being treated poorly elsewhere. They think, 'Wow! This is possible. I was not expecting things to be this good.' That's an immediate win for you and your staff.

—Billy Griffin, Founder and President, New Moon Natural Foods

It is extremely important. If employer doesn't offer paid sick leave and worker is sick, they can't go to work or are forced to go while sick and then infect the rest of workplace. If they have childcare responsibility and schools are out or other issues, they are forced to make a difficult choice. If you can help them avoid making these awful decisions, you then attract and retain terrific people you might otherwise lose.

—Dave Bolotsky, CEO of Uncommon Goods

It's not just moral, it's smart- if we better understand and address the needs of our workforce, they will better connect with clients and engage fully in their work. We see the data and the business case for it over and over and over.

—Brigid Shulte, Director of the Better Life Lab at New America; host of the Better Life Lab podcast; author of *Overwhelmed*

If you truly care about employees as people, they will care about you. It's not necessarily programs and policies- it's creating that underpinning of mutual support that makes people willing to go extra mile for you.

—Doreen Anthony, Vice President, People and Culture at Concord Management Services

If you can provide the feeling of belonging, the personal and psychological safety that encourages employees to bring their whole self to work- I truly believe it affects your culture and the level of employee engagement. If you only recognize 60% of who they are, you only get 60% of them. You don't get the 100% or everything you can. The more people can feel like people at work the better.

—Robert Russo, Executive Director- Human Resources at Bristol-Myers Squibb

It is so important- You can't risk not supporting employees as whole people in this day and age and this rapidly changing environment. You already have a challenge to find the right people. You need a comprehensive talent strategy that is diverse and inclusive. You need to think out of the box- that's how you get a reputation among job candidates.

—Mika Cross, Workforce Transformation Strategist; formerly at US Dept. of Labor and US Office of Personnel Management

Being competitive in total compensation and employee wellbeing is so important, especially in local markets where talent can be scarce. This means flexible work arrangements and mental health support for employees. If you treat employees as whole people, they can bring their whole selves both to work and to home. That's how you build a brand as an employer.

—Bill Plastine, Head of Employee Development and Performance at BASF

It's vital and it's up to us as employers. Employers should look at the totality of wellbeing options- how do I help my employees be the most well they can be in all spheres in their lives. Offer a range of support so everyone can feel they belong in the workplace. The benefits for employers are that their people will have more energy, discretionary effort, and loyalty. They want to work for great workplaces.

—Elizabeth Hall, Vice President, Employee Experience at Cambia Health Solutions

Here's something new in last few years. Especially if you are a consumer-facing brand, people care about what you are doing for employees. If you are not doing right by employees, you will be called out by consumers. And if you act as if you care, but your actions don't match up- it's a double-whammy.

—Julia Beck, Founder and CEO of the It's Working Project

If you have an employee who is having a conflict in the different spheres in their lives, it makes them less happy and productive. As much as possible, employers need to see where they can have a positive impact. Sometimes you can't, but those conversations need to happen.

—Amy Beacom, Founder and CEO of the
Center for Parental Leave Leadership

We asked our members [small businesses throughout the State of New Jersey] what their greatest tool was for employee recruitment and retention. 63% said it was creating a positive flexible work culture- this was their most important and most cost-effective retention tool. It has gone from a 'nice thing to do' to an imperative for companies both large and small- it's now a necessary way to compete for talent.

—John Sarno, President of The Employers Association of New Jersey

You have to understand it should be all on the table. The generation now and coming up the pipeline, as well as everyone going through pandemic is considering all the variables in their lives at the same time.

—Lauren Smith Brody, Author of *The Fifth Trimester*,
Founder of Fifth Trimester Consulting

Now more than ever, employers need to recognize that people bring their whole selves to work, and need to address the whole person.

—Dan Domenech, CHRO, HPE Financial Services at Hewlett
Packard Enterprise

Even in the best of times, employee health, wellness, and wellbeing are critical for an engaged, creative workforce. Now think about how people are juggling so many things. The vast majority of our workforce cannot do their best work unless we rethink how employees can be successful.

—Alyssa Westring, associate professor of management at
DePaul University; Co-author of *Parents Who Lead*

If you are dealing with things in your personal life, it can be distracting and prevent you from bringing your whole self to work. If your employer can help with that, employees can be at work in a better, more focused, more engaged state of mind. It is fundamental.

—Eric Williams, Campaign Director of the
New York Paid Leave Coalition; Consultant

Building a culture of trust is more important than any single policy. It's a two-way relationship. If you go above and beyond for an employee, it comes back to you. If employees go above and beyond for you, it comes back to them. Freedom, flexibility and responsibility flows both ways.

—Chris Geschickter, CHRO at Johnstone Supply

People are the base asset of the company, and you want to support them to get the best out of them.

—Karen Cardona, People and Culture Coordinator at Convene

I see a direct link between companies and leaders who had these [whole-person] values. They were 10 steps ahead in their thinking when Covid hit and everything unfolded. This is the future, and more and more employers need to recognize this.

—Jessica DeGroot, Founder and President of Thirdpath Institute

There's much more awareness of the fact that employees have lives outside the office and employers had been trying to pretend this wasn't the case. But now employers understand that they have to address family and other issues, because these affect customer service, productivity, turnover, and engagement.

—Cynthia Calvert, Principal at Workforce 21C

It's always been important but is now so much more visible. It brings reputational advantages to companies- from prospective employees and customers- when you put good policies in place and can verify they are implemented as advertised.

—Vicki Shabo, Senior Fellow,
Paid Leave Policy and Strategy at New America

I would sum it up this way- just be a human being. People don't just exist at work or in the store. I don't. They don't. If you are aware of this, you can support employees as people and in their lives outside of work. This allows employees to feel better about themselves at work, and they pass that on to how they treat customers, and how they pitch in to help their fellow employees. It benefits everyone.

—Tom Prendergast, Co-owner of Jugtown Country Store

Anything in the workplace that can help an employee fulfill all of their roles, it means they can be more engaged, productive and loyal- because they can then bring their whole selves to work. They feel they can live their full life thanks to their relationship with this company.

—Stephanie Smith, Vice President & CHRO at DePaul University

For the long history of work, work and life were considered very separate, and employers didn't think of you outside of work hours. This model is no longer an effective one. You have to keep in mind work-life friction and challenges. This doesn't just help employees but also helps employers have more satisfied, focused, effective workers if you can acknowledge the whole person.

—Brie Reynolds, Career Development Manager at FlexJobs

Employees can spend their life thriving or struggling in key areas of their lives. We have to ask how we can help all of us get to thriving in all those areas. If you think about, and provide a wide range of support, for the employee to thrive as a whole person, then the value proposition goes off the chart. Just on health care spending alone- those who thrive average

$4000 a year, those struggling average over $12000. And this doesn't even get to the benefits of engagement and productivity.

—Tony Bridwell, CHRO at Ryan, LLC; author of *The ChangeMaker*

AN INTRODUCTION TO THE WHOLE-PERSON WORKPLACE

THIS IS NOT THE BOOK I INTENDED TO WRITE.

THROUGHOUT LATE 2019, I was busy working on a book proposal, outline, and sample chapters for a book I was calling *The Family-Forward Workplace*. It would be based on my work as a business school professor, work-family scholar, and organizational consultant, as well as the workshops and sessions I've held with working parents around the country. The book was going to guide employers, large and small, in helping their employees rise to their work-life challenges. It was going to demonstrate the business case for- and help employers implement- robust telecommuting and work-from-home policies.

In early 2020, I signed my book deal- things were going exactly according to plan! Surely nothing could go wrong...

Then came March 2020, when the reality of the Covid pandemic hit the United States. The American working world turned upside down.

I was teaching at my university's partner business school in Paris at the time and was one of those panicked Americans abroad that you may remember seeing on the news streaming into US airports ahead of a hastily-proposed (and then sloppily-retracted) travel ban. My university went fully online, as did a huge percentage of employers.

Pre-Covid, business culture mandated that most employees be at their workplace for their full working hours with very few exceptions and little flexibility- even if this decision didn't always make good business sense. Now, because of Covid, most employers were telling any employee who

I remember!

didn't absolutely, positively have to be at the workplace to work from home instead.

Millions, probably including you, were left to figure out work-family balance, online schooling, a lack of child-care, Zoom etiquette, heightened anxiety, and social isolation- all while setting work-life boundaries, staying connected with coworkers, getting your work done, projecting confidence to your managers, and keeping the dog from barking during your online presentation.

The essential employees who were required to go to work entered a new workplace as well- one with (hopefully) enhanced safety protocols, transformed work processes, and grave anxiety about getting sick and spreading the virus to their loved ones.

Getting through the height of the crisis was no small accomplishment. As author and podcaster Brigid Schulte relayed it to me, "the fact that 41 million employees with young kids and no school or child care have been able to get through Summer 2020 is nothing short of miraculous." Agreed.

So much of the business advice you've seen and read pre-Covid still has relevance, but we are truly in a new world. So much received wisdom has been overthrown. So many new challenges and opportunities have emerged. Workplaces have changed- and many of these changes will persist. Decades from now, we will see so many aspects of society as "pre-Covid" or "post-Covid."

Covid changed the world, the workplace, and even this book. I had to throw out *The Family-Forward Workplace*. A book focused on helping employers implement work-from-home had become obsolete before it was half-way written. In light of, and smack dab in the middle of the Covid crisis, I started over with a whole new approach to help employers navigate their way through the changes to their structures, cultures, and employee policies brought on by the pandemic.

Also, after interviewing over four dozen subject-matter experts- CEOs, HR professionals, small business owners, advocates, academics and other thought leaders- I learned my prior approach was too narrow. Working parents aren't the only employees who need support. Being "family forward" was too limiting and too limited an approach.

Something bigger is needed. The way forward is not just through telecommuting, parental leave, and a finite set of "family-forward" policies. In the post-Covid world, life and work have become enmeshed like never before. Business success now requires something more transformative.

WELCOME TO *THE WHOLE-PERSON WORKPLACE*

Now more than ever, the surest route to success for the widest array of businesses is to change the way we value employees. An employee is not just a piece of organizational machinery to be used for a period of time, paid fairly for their contribution and then sent out the door. Employees are people, with full lives outside of work and, most often, a strong desire to bring many aspects of themselves into the workplace.

Delta Emerson, founder and president of canyouhearus consulting and formerly the President of Global Shared Services at Ryan, LLC, said it best during a Workforce Live! Presentation[2]:

> *We have to realize we get the whole person through the door. We get their backs and their hands and their minds and their hearts, and they're all at different stages in their lives, and we have to make sure we're doing the very best we can to keep them long-term. Because if we do that, they're going to help us succeed.*

If we- employers, managers, human resources professionals, and leaders- view our employees as whole people, it opens up so many avenues for us to support our employees with their life challenges. Yes, this means supporting working parents, especially after birth and during their children's early childhoods. But it also means supporting all employees' needs for psychological well-being and physical safety. It means assisting employees with their full variety of life challenges- financial stability, caring for elderly parents, giving back to the community. It means listening to employee concerns and crafting custom-fit solutions. It means creating a culture in which all employees feel respected, appreciated, and welcomed to bring their full selves to work.

This can seem like an all-encompassing task, but the rewards are worth it. Every single business leader I talked to while researching the book asserted that supporting employees as whole people is the key to long-term, sustainable success. Creating a Whole-Person Workplace helps you attract the best talent, who then stay with you, become increasingly engaged, and treat your customers as whole people as well.

How in a Zoom world?

Finally, we are living through what is perhaps the greatest experiment in workplace transformation and work-life challenge in modern history. It would be a shame to go through all this just to revert to the old way of doing things. We need to take the opportunity through Covid and into the post-Covid work world to manage our companies differently, better, and with the hard-earned recognition that employees are whole people, with a need to be supported as such.

THE TURNING POINT

I'd like to begin *The Whole-Person Workplace* by sharing one of my favorite stories. A story of the very moment when a typical hard-charging workplace- one that employees called "a highly-skilled, well-paid sweatshop"- started their journey to becoming a best-in-class Whole-Person Workplace[3].

In January 2008, Kristi Bryant, a young, whip smart, up-and-coming manager at Ryan LLC walked into CEO G. Brint Ryan's office. She was a rising star at Ryan, someone who seemed ticketed for top management. But the look on Kristi's face gave Brint pause. She approached his desk and said:

I love my job. I love this company. I'm starting a family. Here's my resignation.

Even though Ryan had been financially successful, its intense work culture was threatening its long-term trajectory. In an environment where "long hours were worn like a badge," people like Kristi, who aspired to career success and a fulfilling family life, couldn't see a way to make it work. Something had to change or else so many of Ryan's valuable employees would follow her right out the door.

Flash-forward to today, and thanks to a seven-plus year commitment (and considerable continuous-improvement efforts since then), Ryan has created a workplace that prioritizes both high performance and the long-term well-being of their employees- including the flexibility needed for fulfilling family lives outside of work. Ryan is financially stronger and growing more quickly than ever- because it is now a place where working parents and, indeed, all employees can be successful at work and at home. The kind of Whole-Person Workplace in which the Kristi Bryants of the world thrive.

In fact, thanks to some quick thinking by Brint and his promise to create a Whole-Person Workplace, he was able to convince Kristi to stay on. She is now a high-performing principal who manages two important teams. She remains a strong candidate for top leadership, and she has been able to accelerate her career while also having the time and support she needs to be a great mom to two young children.

Ryan's transformation was not easy. It is the long-term result of a coherent set of workplace improvements, including especially effective approaches to flexible work and performance evaluation. Ryan is now a "results-only work environment," which means that, as long as employees do great work, have happy clients, and receive positive feedback from managers and coworkers, a Ryan employee can do their work from anywhere and at any time. They can leave early, work from home, and leverage technology in a way that upholds high performance and allows them to lead successful lives outside of work.

These changes would not have taken root unless managers and staff throughout Ryan- with the full support and encouragement of the executive suite- created and nourished a culture that values profits, of course, but also truly values its employees as whole people.

In fact, the 2008 Ryan employee survey found that only 42% of employees agreed with the statement, "At Ryan, people are encouraged to balance their work life and their personal life." Now, over 95% agree. Further, their 2019 employee survey shows that 96% of Ryan employees feel engaged at work (and as CHRO Tony Bridwell states, "we're obsessed with reaching the other 4%"), Glassdoor lists G. Brint Ryan as having a 95% personal approval rate and, most impressively, as the #2 most effective CEO during the Covid pandemic[4].

Better still, this improvement never represented a financial trade-off. In 2015, Ryan made its debut on Fortune's list of the Top 100 Companies to Work For[5] and has continued to earn a spot on the list ever since. By any financial measure, they are a much more successful company now than when they started their journey.

EMBRACING WHOLE-PERSON WORKPLACE VALUES

Unlike Brint, you probably have never experienced such a personal epiphany about the business imperative of helping your employees with the challenges they face in their lives.

However, if you are a manager or leader at a demanding workplace, I can almost guarantee that you have lost good people when intense work expectations crashed headlong into employees' desire for a full life outside of work. Instead of striding into the CEO's office, most burned-out employees- who would love to stay but can't see a way to make their employment with you fit with the rest of their lives- simply melt away and find employment elsewhere. There goes your talent, the lifeblood of your company, right out the door.

Every time your employees spend extended hours on high-stress work without the means to alleviate their situations, there is a cost. Every time work comes between a parent and an important family event, commitment ebbs. Missed family dinners, school events, and soccer games prevent employees from being the parents they always wanted to be- and that their kids need them to be.

This is true for all employees- not just working parents. Stressful work demands can crowd out time for dating, a social life, time with older relatives, and opportunities to contribute to communities or to feed personal passions. Even worse, this emotional toll can make our employees less healthy and less able to care for others.

There may be short-term benefits to long, unrelenting hours and high-pressure environments. However, over time, these short-term gains bring with them even larger losses, for both employers and employees. HR thought leader Josh Bersin details the direct and indirect costs of turnover[6]:

- » Cost of hiring a new person (advertising, interviewing, screening, hiring)
- » Cost of onboarding a new person (training, management time)
- » Lost productivity (a new person may take 1-2 years to reach the productivity of an existing person)
- » Lost engagement (other employees who see high turnover disengage and lose productivity)
- » Customer service and errors (new employees take longer and are often less adept at solving problems). In healthcare, for example, this may result in higher error rates, illness, and lawsuits
- » Training cost (over 2-3 years you likely invest 10-20% of an employee's salary or more in training, that is gone)
- » Cultural impact (whenever someone leaves others ask "why?")

Bersin also asserts that, "people are what we call an 'appreciating asset.' The longer we stay with an organization the more productive we get-we learn the systems, we learn the products, and we learn how to work together."

When a valuable employee quits, they take with them all the time and energy you've spent developing them, plus all of their future contributions, plus all of their internal and external networks. The employees who stay become even more over-worked and burned-out, losing engagement and commitment to your firm while greatly increasing their risk for physical and emotional problems. And, worst of all, over time, these losses accumulate into a well-earned reputation as an employer at which the best talent no longer wants to work.

These costs are all real, but employees aren't just valuable assets. They are people. Employers owe it to the whole people who work for them to provide an environment where they can thrive, both at work and in the rest of their lives. It is both the right thing to do and smart business to respect employees as whole people.

The good news is that many leading companies, even those in competitive industries, have taken steps to become Whole-Person Workplaces. You have, no doubt, already read about lots of well-publicized efforts from large companies in the tech and financial sectors- industries marked by a war for rare and valuable talent among a relatively small set of competitors. But these employers, with all of their reputations and resources, only tell part of the story.

The fact is, companies large and small, in the widest array of industries, and with employees ranging from scientists and MBAs to hourly retail and fast food, have developed ways to value and support their employees while also achieving financial success[7].

Every Whole-Person Workplace has a different starting point and a different set of challenges. They each address their challenges in ways that reflect their values, their business imperatives, and the unique aspects of their work cultures. Some proudly promote specific family-supportive policies, like parental leave and telecommuting. Others reinvigorated employee wellness and employee assistance programs. Some fixed problems in their approaches to performance management, compensation, and employee recognition. Others have taken a more comprehensive approach by establishing cultural values, providing leadership training, and unleashing the potential of employee empowerment.

In many of the companies we'll discuss, skeptical managers initially saw financial success and well-being as opposing forces. However, they have since come away convinced that valuing both profits and people is synergistic, and the best means for sustained success. As one example, at the 2014 White House Summit for Working Families, EY CEO Mark Weinberger asserted that, "addressing work-family issues is a no brainer. We don't need any more economic analysis to know its importance[8]."

Throughout *The Whole-Person Workplace*, I will share stories and provide guidance on how you can implement a custom-fit version of these ideas into your workplace. I'll share practical advice for leaders and top management, human resources professionals, small business owners and supervisors. These lessons can be applied in smaller units, departments, not-for profits, or any other team-based setting. No matter where you are situated in the organizational chart, there are many things you can do to improve productivity and employee well-being within your sphere of influence. This book can be your guide.

Finally, this book can also be your shield. There are still some "old-school" managers and leaders who don't yet recognize the importance of a Whole-Person approach. They may believe employee supportiveness is a "nice-to-have," but not nearly as important as other aspects of management. They may focus on up-front costs as opposed to long-term benefits. Post-Covid, they may be itching to get their full workplaces back at the office "where they belong", regardless of how successfully they navigated work-from-home just months earlier.

In my years of experience researching this topic and working with managers, I'm increasingly convinced that an approach to management that values employees as Whole People is not just ethical, nice, or the "right way to treat people." It is good business in the long term to invest in your employees, helping them rise to the major challenges in their lives. It is good business to create a workplace in which people can be their best selves at work and still have the time and energy to have a full life outside of work.

Billy Griffin, founder and president of New Moon Natural Foods, makes the case better than I can:

> *The thing that elevates this from a mere strategy to a passion is belief in the power of business to amplify what's in our heart. We have it in our capacity to use the power of business to benefit our fellow humans as well as the bottom line. They're not mutually exclusive. And the place to start is with the very people who make the business function in the first place.*

The fact you are reading this book means you probably feel the same way. This book will help you make the business case in your company.

HOW *THE WHOLE PERSON WORKPLACE* WILL UNFOLD

In Chapter 1, we'll begin by discussing changes to the workplace due to the Covid pandemic. Many of these changes, such as more expansive use of communication technology and work-from-home, are here to stay. Further, many companies are now more intentional about the demands they put on employees to be physically present and co-located. There are also subtler post-Covid changes; for example, we've now had a look inside the homes and family lives of many of our coworkers, blurring the lines between work and home, colleague and friend. In this chapter, a wide array of business leaders share their ideas on which workplace changes will persist, which will revert, and why so many workplace changes that they were "forced into" wound up leading to creative solutions and new opportunities.

In Chapter 2, we'll discuss workplace flexibility in more detail. Now that there's proof that so many employees can get their work done outside of the office and at times other than regular hours, more workplaces will continue with flex. But the success of flex depends on whether it is embraced or merely tolerated, and we'll discuss how to make flex work well, convincing even the "old school" skeptics of its merits. We also need to distinguish between tasks that work well at a distance, tasks that require in-person interaction, and how we can bridge any gaps between them. We'll see how Flexjobs.com, which was founded as a fully-remote workforce, developed creative solutions to the challenges of hiring, onboarding, collaborating, and celebrating success. Finally, we emphasize that workplaces need to retain a culture of flexibility and resilience for when the next disruption takes place.

In Chapters 3 and 4, we'll focus more directly on new parents, a slice of our workforce that face the highest levels of work-life conflict and are deserving of large- and small-scale supports from their employers, managers, and coworkers. In chapter 3, we'll discuss how to craft parental leave policies that assist new parents, while respecting coworkers and ensuring continuity of performance. This way, parental leave works for everyone. In Chapter 4, we'll discuss the range of supports that are particularly valued by working parents during early childhood. We'll cover how to re-integrate employees coming back from leave, provide physical accommodations for new moms, and how we can ease the stress caused by often-inconsistent and all-too-expensive child-care.

New parents aren't the only care-givers, and they aren't the only employees who need support. In Chapter 5, we'll discuss such topics as support for elder care, financial planning, continuing education, and respecting time for life outside of work. We'll also discuss the power of supporting employees in their outside interests, and especially their desire to contribute to their communities. Finally, we'll note that the best way to address the wide variety of employee challenges is to continually engage, listen, and creatively respond with custom-fit solutions.

In Chapters 6 and 7, we'll explore how becoming a Whole-Person Workplace doesn't necessarily require new programs. In fact, one of the most powerful ways to support employees is to revisit how you manage hiring, new employee orientation, work-hour expectations, performance evaluations, compensation, and core benefits like health insurance. We'll discuss how Ryan transformed its performance management process away from a focus on hours worked, and towards performance on key metrics- enabling employees to work more flexibly that ever before. We'll also see how Gravity Payment's commitment to a $70k minimum salary not only resulted in a happier and more engaged workforce, but also a workforce that was now able to buy houses, save for education, and start families.

A Whole-Person approach also needs to address the physical person. In Chapter 8, we'll focus on wellness programs and explore why employee health and safety are so strongly linked with engagement and performance. We'll discuss both physical and mental health, as well as a wide range of benefits and services one can provide to reduce the stress many of our employees carry. We'll profile several compelling examples of workplaces that implemented successful, comprehensive approaches to employee wellness.

Chapter 9 pulls many of the concepts from the prior chapters together. After all, a Whole-Person Workplace is not simply a collection of one-off initiatives and programs. It is a set of intentional, strategic choices about what a workplace values and how these values are enacted into a culture in which all employees can thrive. We'll spotlight leading Whole-Person Workplaces known for their progressive work cultures. We'll hear from top managers and CHROs about how to embed Whole-Person values into culture and how you can get started with this transformational process.

Chapter 10 reviews our content by presenting ideas for how all the different audiences for this book- leaders, managers, HR professionals, small business owners, employees, and job-seekers- can implement the concepts we've explored together. This advice can help you get started making your workplace one in which employees are valued as whole people.

Finally, in the Afterword, we recognize that Whole-Person Workplaces must provide fair opportunity and an environment where everyone can feel comfortable bringing their whole selves to work. Diversity and inclusion have always been important, but the recent attention paid to racial justice and gender equity has brought these issues to the forefront.

CHAPTER 1 – HOW COVID CHANGED THE WORKPLACE

IT HAS BEEN SAID that adversity builds character. For so many of us in so many walks of life, Covid has delivered considerable adversity. Covid is an incredibly destructive force that killed hundreds of thousands and made life harder for millions more. There's no sugar-coating its devastating effects.

It is equally true that adversity reveals character. No matter their stated values, the true values of employers and managers become more evident in a crisis. Workplaces that value their employees as whole people responded in ways to not only protect their finances, but also take care of its employees. For essential employees, this may have meant temporary hazard pay, improved workplace safety measures, and support for mental health. For non-essential employees, this meant an embrace of flexible and remote work, along with work-life supports.

Workplace strategist Mika Cross, who worked on several federal agencies' response to Covid, advocates putting whole-person workplace values front and center when responding to this or any other crisis:

5 years later, what do we want to say about how we supported people working through this? That's a good start.

Sara Sutton and Karen LaGraff of Flexjobs[1] add:

Employees always remember how they were treated during times of crisis and how leaders handled the situation.

Because of Covid, many organizations have re-examined their priorities and enacted policies that they would never have previously considered. These changes have required creativity, and some presented opportunities while others brought about hardships. The best employers kept one eye on their finances, but also focused on how they could help their employees through these difficult times.

Now, as we move forward, employers need to determine which elements of their emergency reaction worked well and should be retained; which elements no longer fit their or their employees' needs; and which elements- for better or for worse- are simply new realities.

I'm writing this chapter in Fall 2020 with the understanding that the situation is fluid and unpredictable. Perhaps many aspects of our society and workplaces can return to semi-normal by mid-2021, but it is also possible we will face a deadly situation for far longer. Employees' need for childcare and work from home will differ based on geography and the decisions of thousands of independent school districts. Perhaps an effective vaccine is found and distributed soon; maybe we never get a handle on the virus. So much depends on national, state, and local leadership, on how our citizenry reacts going forward, and especially on how the spread of a novel virus continues to unfold.

With all this uncertainty, we don't know exactly how Covid-related workplace changes will play out. However, it is clear that those who remain adaptable and nimble while leading with employee-centered values will come out of this better than those with closed minds and narrow perspectives.

How you remain flexible and express whole-person workplace values is yours to decide based on your particular situation. However, pre-Covid business as usual is no longer an option. In this book, we'll cover a wide variety of ways you can make whole person workplace values real. These will help you examine the needs of your changing workforce not only in terms of Covid, but also in terms of the many business challenges you face.

I asked every expert I interviewed for this book about their experiences managing through the Spring-Summer 2020 height of the Covid crisis and their thoughts about what might come next in "the new abnormal." This chapter is organized around the clear themes that emerged from their responses.

These themes include:

» The Covid crisis accelerated many changes that were already underway

    » The relationship between employer and employee has been changed- in some ways for the better and some ways for the worse

    » Work is increasingly separated from the workplace

    » Telework and many other workplace changes are here to stay

» Employers and coworkers have gotten a more personal glimpse into and a better understanding of each other's personal lives and challenges

    » This has reinforced the need to be more intentional about how we communicate and handle the interpersonal aspects of work

    » The crisis raised the importance of physical and especially psychological wellness, motivating many employers to do more for their employees in these areas

» Employers that already had whole-person workplace values and embraced flexibility are better able to adapt to this crisis and to future challenges

THE GREAT ACCELERATION

I am not the first to point out that the Covid pandemic has accelerated many positive and negative trends in society, culture, technology, and business that were already underway. For example, e-commerce, streaming digital, political polarization, income inequality, work-from-home, telemedicine, media consolidation, and homeschooling had all been on the rise in the decade leading up to the crisis.

Similarly, many industries, sectors, and companies that had already been under stress are now pushed closer to the breaking point. Examples include shopping malls, movie theaters, vacation time-shares, gyms, smaller private colleges, and live theater (these last two are particularly personal to me as a professor married to a theater actress/director). Other elements of business, such as shared office spaces, business travel, and international supply chains are being fully reconsidered.

Some aspects of the employer-employee dynamic have tilted away from workers. Many employers have gone out of business or had to greatly restrict their activity. This has meant layoffs, furloughs, part-time work, and other cutbacks. Employees face a difficult labor market. John Sarno, president of the Employers Association of New Jersey notes that:

> We've gone from a nearly full-employment economy, in which the challenges for employers were dramatically different- including recruiting and retaining skilled employees in an environment of extremely low labor availability. Many employers believed in being employee-friendly, but others only did so because of market demands.
>
> But now with many businesses flat-out closed, and millions unemployed, the incentive for employers isn't the same. Some will be back to 'take it or leave it' or 'when I say jump, you say how high' now that they have the upper hand.

Amy Beacom of the Center for Parental Leave Leadership sees things similarly:

> We went from great employment numbers to the worst we've seen. With so many people laid off, the calculus for finding and keeping people is different. I don't think it's a great long-term

business strategy, but the imperative to treat employees well so as to retain them may change.

To some degree in the short-term, employers can probably get away with offering lower pay, fewer benefits, and less personal consideration. Unfortunately, this is the new reality for many workers and will be until the economy rebounds. However, thankfully, in many workplaces, employers are attempting to meet employee needs.

Many "essential worker" workplaces, such as warehouses, hospitals, factories, and public works facilities still rely upon pre-Covid staffing levels and workflow. Even so, in many of these settings, there have already been significant changes to workplaces[2] and safety procedures[3] including:

» Reduced overall building capacity

» Barriers and physical markers to maintain social distance

» Mask requirements

» Greatly increased surface cleaning and sanitation

» Improvements to air filtration and airflow

» Separation of desks, cubicles, and work stations with Plexiglas

» Temperature checks, health "check-in" apps, semi-regular Covid testing

» Changes to how employees enter, exit, and move throughout workplaces

» A retrenchment away from open-office plans and shared workspaces

» Limiting the number of people in common areas, such as lunch areas and conference rooms (even using infrared sensors to monitor this[4])

» Fewer large-group meetings

Billy Griffin, founder and president of New Moon Natural Foods, who employs about 90 mostly hourly employees, sees many workplace safety changes as good things to retain going forward:

During the pandemic, we discovered we could do things to keep staff healthier. Looking ahead, let's do things like cleaning and sanitizing high-touch areas in the store all the time, especially in employee spaces. It's not that hard, probably one employee and forty-five minutes in a day. Door handles and registers and the phones in the office get touched by lots of employees, and there will always be cold and flu season. We can keep people healthier, pandemic or not.

SEPARATING WORK FROM THE WORKPLACE

On a more positive note, Delta Emerson of canyouhearus consulting states that, at least in terms of workplace flexibility, "It's a whole new world. It's like we fast-forwarded what we hoped companies would do." With improvements to communication technology, wide availability of internet and Wi-Fi, and the digitization of business documentation, it has become far more possible for employees to work remotely than ever before.

Beth Rivera, the CHRO of Uncommon Goods, details how their workplace adjusted to Covid:

The biggest change for us is remote work. For us, we are based in one office- one of the reasons we invested in this awesome facility was to build community and collaboration. Now, we are starting to see people being more productive working from home, and, of course, we are concerned about their health and comfort coming back. Flexibility and the desire to work remotely will only increase. Many employees are really liking this with the cost savings, no commuting time, and quality of life. This will change how we work. We can't just say, 'let's have a meeting'. We need to be more creative in our collaboration.

Stephanie Smith, Vice President & CHRO of DePaul University discusses changes to her workplace:

In mid-March, we had to disband what we were doing and everyone had to stay home unless they were an essential employee. Most of us worked from home regardless of what we were doing and we figured it out. Operations went on. For my HR team, I think we were more productive. We had fewer distractions, made the most of our meetings, and organized them only when we needed them. I think that's the case for a lot of workplaces.

Before Covid, we of course made exceptions, but they had to prove how someone can still be productive if not fully present. Now, it's the opposite. I ask managers, 'What is your compelling business case to go back to campus? To make people return when they've been working remotely successfully?' Pre-Covid, they would have looked at me like I had two heads for saying something like this. It's a total change in point of view.

I'm heading our task force for long-term remote work. There will be a sizeable number of units with remote modality for a long time, and even those who come back will come back in hybrid modality. Few units, if any, will have everyone physically coming back to work.

As Smith's quote illustrates, some workplaces have decided that a significant percentage of their employees can work remotely. Most will embrace some combination of remote and in-person work. For example, some will allow individual work to be done remotely and then reimagine their workspaces to prioritize only those activities in which employees need to be together, excising the rest of one's real estate footprint[5]. According to William Aruda[6]:

Once there are medical breakthroughs like treatments and vaccines, offices will be more about interaction and community than about heads-down focus on individual productivity.

Conference rooms, meeting spaces and video studios will take up a lot of office space. The workplace will become a far more social environment, not a 'lock myself in the office' scenario. It will be designed to foster and promote interaction and community engagement- taking advantage of the times talent is collocated in one place.

Getting from the present to a new workplace reality will take a lot of skill and nuance. Leaders need to carefully plan and involve HR, IT, facilities, and legal teams- and of course employees- in figuring out their new normal. Professor and work-life author Alyssa Westring notes that:

The complexity of bringing people back to the office is another component. It's a legal and HR nightmare- many may prefer to keep employees out of the office and then consider whether they need to use the space they have, with their new realization they don't always need people co-located.

John Sarno reports on a survey of EANJ's membership, which consists of hundreds of small and mid-sized employers in New Jersey:

60% [of member companies] sent their workers home. However, until there is a huge remission or a vaccine or return to a normal business climate, things are not going back to before. We're in remote work for the foreseeable future. Only 14% of members want everyone back, but don't know when that can happen- and only when employees feel safe. I think a lot of these changes will be permanent.

We may be in a transitional period for some time. However, many organizations have either accepted or embraced new ways of working. Many of these changes, including at least a partial, fluid separation between work and workplace, should endure. We'll fully cover workplace flexibility and remote work, as well as the factors that make these options more or less appropriate for different work settings, in the next chapter.

BUSINESS BECAME MORE PERSONAL

Consider the following quotes:

> *One good side of this situation is that we got to know people on more personal level. We can see your daughter in background and take a minute to chat about her skirt- and that's totally ok. Used to be- 'get out,' now it's 'don't worry about it!' and 'what's your daughter's name?'*

—Ginny Kissling, Global President and COO of Ryan, LLC

> *Personal lives are much more visible than before. Newer generations were already comfortable with this, but now everyone is experiencing it. Now we see our coworker as a person, mom, dad, not just as a worker. We will account for them as a whole person. Especially seeing how people are working through challenging times with young kids, home schooling. We even see leaders and colleagues struggling... And it's ok for it to be a struggle because it shows how dedicated you are and that you are human. Every parent on conference call while doing dishes sees the value of these things. At least, now our eyes are open to what people go through with work and family.*

—Lauren Smith Brody, author <u>The Fifth Trimester</u>

> *Covid took everything out of the closet.*

—Julia Beck, founder and CEO of the It's Working Project

Because many of us worked from home during the Spring and Summer without schools or child-care, we were faced with an impossible juggle. Further, because lots of us worked with videoconferencing, we all put some of our lives on display while also getting a glimpse into the home and personal lives of our coworkers. Ironically, by working at a distance, many of us became closer to our colleagues. Lisa Evans of Conagra Foods notes:

My team was pretty close to begin with- about 11 of us in 2 major cities. We always worked well with this geographic spread. But now, we put more effort into our Microsoft Teams meetings, our social hours, and our communication is better. We spend more time to get to know each other as people and not just the work. We see the dog walk by and the kid come in. We get a window into each other's lives.

Over time, this should create better interpersonal dynamics at work, especially as managers see how well their teams perform even with all of the work-life challenges they face. This can prove transformational. As Amy Beacom, founder of the Center for Parental Leave Leadership, states:

The story we've told employees forever is that anything personal stays home, we don't want to hear about it. Now we are flipping that switch. As leaders, we are here to help you take care of things and provide you resources that enable you to be more productive, even if this means a more flexible approach.

Another effect of widespread remote work had been the recognition that we used to waste a lot of time with meetings and long hours. In many workplaces, managers and employees are more intentional about the use of time, and especially about time spent in meetings. Mika Cross explains:

Everyone is considering how to extend remote work post-pandemic. This is a huge paradigm shift. Workplaces are rethinking which parts of work to prioritize- high-level versus low-impact work. What is the real necessity for a meeting, for people to be together to work? If not needed, how can we handle it differently?

In some ways, this intentionality has improved organizational communication. Dave Bolotsky, CEO of Uncommon Goods:

During Covid-related remote work, we in leadership host weekly video updates to communicate about what's going on in various departments, take questions, and hear employee concerns. About 50% of employees attend these- more than we could have had in any individual meeting before.

This intentionality can even extend to relationships with clients and outside stakeholders, leading to creative approaches to connection when you can't easily have in-person business lunches. Ginny Kissling of Ryan, LLC explains:

We've done fun virtual client events. One was 'Zoom Bloom' where we sent clients flowers and then offered a virtual class run by a floral designer who led them through making their own arrangements. Also, a virtual wine tasting where we sent them wine tasting kits, a few bottles of wine and then had an expert lead them through a tasting.

Finally, the window we have into our employees' lives has demonstrated that, for many, things are not going well[7]. Many employees are drowning at work-from-home, especially those with young children. Some feel very isolated by remote work, and, of course, some are facing significant financial hardships. Many have dealt with family members getting sick or living with the constant anxiety for the safety of their loved ones. This is especially true for front-line, essential workers and their families. Many who care for aging relatives may be even more stressed.

Tom Prendergast, co-owner of Jugtown Country Store, a small convenience store in the White Mountains of New Hampshire, demonstrates his care for the safety of his employees:

Especially during Covid, we have to pay attention to their safety, wellbeing and peace of mind. Everyone who works goes home and has a life and interacts with other people. Coming in to work for not so much money, and taking those risks home to their loved ones is not easy. So their safety needs to be our concern and we need to respect their well-being. We stand up for employees by making customers wear masks- and making them leave if they won't. I couldn't, in good conscience, have them breathing on employees.

All of these hardships are now (or at least should be on) employers' radars. The need to support the physical and especially the psychological and emotional wellness of employees is particularly urgent. We'll cover wellness programs in great detail in Chapter 8. Elizabeth Hall, Vice President, Employee Experience at Cambia Health Solutions thoughtfully highlights how they've adapted their wellness programs for the current moment:

We have long offered a wide-range of wellness initiatives at the workplace, but during this time of remote work, our Wellness and Learning & Development teams in HR worked together on something more holistic. We had already become increasingly aware of mind-body connection. Whatever challenges people had pre-Covid, Covid has intensified these. Mental and physical health, we need to address both. Now, we hold webinar-based training for teams on resilience and hold online fitness classes twice a day. We have regular webinars on healthy eating with guest chef, and half-hour online yoga classes with a live instructor. During Covid, we've been more creative in our interventions to help employees stay well when their regular options may not be available.

WHOLE-PERSON WORKPLACES ADAPTED BETTER

I agree with Jessica DeGroot, founder of Thirdpath Institute, in her observation regarding employers that adapted better and worse during the Covid crisis:

I saw a direct link between companies and leaders who had the right values and their ability to manage. They were 10 steps ahead in their thinking when everything unfolded. It was the difference between 'O God, how will this work?' versus 'How can we make this work?' It was already part of their DNA.

Julia Beck goes into more detail in a recent article for HBR.org.[8]

She describes how employers with employee-oriented cultures exhibited qualities that are helping them get through the pandemic. What separates these employers is that they already had the capacity to listen to and trust employees, create community at work, and respect the many roles that employees take on outside of work.

Because they already did these things well, they were able to adapt quickly to successful remote work, support employees through difficulties, maintain personal connections even at a distance, and unleash individual creativity in responding to the crisis. These Whole-Person Workplaces are positioned for long-term success after the crisis and are well-adapted to the next emergency. Here are a few examples from business leaders I spoke with that reinforce Beck's observations:

> *We already had our result-only work environment, widespread use of flexibility, and experience measuring results instead of time at work. We were well set up for this. Many other companies who were not there had a lot to do in order to recover.*
>
> —Delta Emerson, former President of
> Global Shared Services at Ryan, LLC.

> *At Concord, we were founded with work from home right at the onset. Everyone has laptops, VPNs, Wi-Fi. We always knew that, you know, sometimes it snows or there are other reasons the office can close. We had already proved we could work remotely. This helped up persevere through the pandemic.*
>
> —Doreen Anthony, VP, People and Culture at
> Concord Management Services

We already had a culture of flexibility, and this gave up lots of options. Not that it was easy to adjust, especially that we have lots of different types of employees- corporate offices, support services, hourly retail, pharmacists. We had to talk to and address them all. But we started from a place that was flexible and agile, which made it better.

—HR Executive at national pharmacy and drug store chain

Workplaces that already valued employees as whole people allowed for work flexibility and provided employees the time they needed to attend to their life challenges were many steps ahead. They didn't need to figure out how to trust employees, help them work together, and respond to the stressors they faced. It was already how they operated. Importantly, they already built a culture in which employees did their best to take care of each other and work hard for the company. Other workplaces had to scramble for solutions. The adversity of the Covid crisis revealed the character of employers all over the country.

Further, as Jessica DeGroot correctly points out, "we may recover from the pandemic, but we could have another shock. Our world is so interconnected, there could be another crisis in ten years. We'll need to stay nimble." Becoming a Whole-Person Workplace will help you adapt to the next emergency.

Finally, Whole-Person Workplaces embrace the positive side of change. Elizabeth Hall of Cambia Health Solutions demonstrates the potential for optimism going forward:

I hope there's no setback. I don't want to go back to the workplace as normal. I want to go forward to something new and great. If 99% of our workforce is successfully working from home, we can do that going forward.

Looking to the future, I see flex all around. As a Northwest employer, we can look at talent all over the country in a way we haven't before- looking at a larger pool and the best talent regardless of US geography. That's exciting! It's exciting to think of your workplace as collaborative hub, and to work less hierarchically and more autonomously. With more choice on where, when and how people work- do I travel to the main location, a local hub, or my home office? Giving employees that freedom gets them to whole new level of work-life navigation. The more we can offer, the more everyone can get what they need.

THE FINAL WORD

The Covid pandemic changed the workplace, in some ways for the better. Employers who embrace Whole-Person Workplace values adapted more quickly to new realities. By embracing changes to workplace design, enacting flexible and remote work, and applying a better understanding of employees' personal lives and challenges, yours can become a workplace that helps its employees thrive and, as a result, succeeds in the long run. Most importantly, you will be able to look back in 5 years and be proud of how you supported employees through this crisis.

IDEAS AND ADVICE

» The Covid pandemic has challenged employers to adapt to new circumstances, balancing business imperatives with the care and well-being of employees. Employers need to consider a wide array of creative approaches and ways of working that they would not have considered even a short time ago.

» Among the most important changes is the widespread use of remote work, which allows for new ways of working and for a window into the personal lives and work-life challenges our employees face. Adaptable employers see the opportunity in remote work.

» Covid has also increased the stressors our employees face, making it more urgent to support their physical and psychological wellness.

» Covid has also necessitated many changes to the workplace, especially those concerning health and safety.

» Employers that exhibited Whole-Person Workplace values before the crisis were better able to adapt, work flexibly, and assure employee engagement by addressing their concerns. Further, Whole-Person values can help employers adapt to future challenges in a way that promotes both employee wellbeing and financial success.

CHAPTER 2 – GETTING THE MOST OUT OF WORKPLACE FLEXIBILITY

FOR THE PAST SEVERAL MONTHS, I've gotten together for Thursday night "Zoom happy hours" with several of my college friends. These calls have been great for morale during the social distancing era, and they have enabled us to spend more time together than we have since our long-ago graduation.

One of the primary topics we discuss is how we are dealing with work-from-home and online school for our kids. My one friend, a NYC law partner who lives with his wife and two teenage daughters in Long Island, is "totally on board for the work from home revolution. I don't have my long commute every day, can have dinner with my family every night, and spend much more time with my daughters." He feels as if he is serving his clients as well as he ever has, even if he spends perhaps too much time on zoom meetings and conference calls.

Another college buddy works in financial services in the greater Boston area, and he is desperate to go back to the office. He has two daughters under 5 and lives about ten minutes from work. Through the height of the pandemic, he was 24/7 with his wife, mother-in-law, and his two delightful but exuberant girls. He confessed he was very frustrated by having to work completely from home and wished he could go back to the office- both for some quiet time and for the social interaction. By the time I submitted this manuscript, his employer has not let employees return to the office. Anyone with boisterous young children can sympathize.

As we saw in the previous chapter, remote work is here to stay. Many companies who would have never offered flexibility before 2020 will probably maintain it in some form. Even pre-Covid, telework was becoming far more common. In fact, over the past decade, the number of workplaces offering remote work nearly doubled[1]. In firms without formal policies in place, many more employees were able to make use of informal and ad-hoc forms of flexibility. A pre-Covid Working Mother Research Institute survey[2] of office-based employees showed that:

» While only 29% of respondents had regularly scheduled flextime/flexplace arrangements, 66% stated they can use flex when they need to. This "as needed" flexibility was the preferred work schedule of a plurality of the respondents- as opposed to formal work-from-home days or full-time work from home.

» 73% were happy with the extent to which they were able to work from home.

» 78% stated that they were at least somewhat comfortable using flexibility.

» 62% said their employers encourage the use of flexibility to at least some extent.

» Those who said their employers encouraged flexibility stated that they were happier, healthier, and more fulfilled at work.

» By huge margins, employees believed that work flexibility helped them be more productive, happier, less stressed, more motivated at work, more effective at home, and more committed to their employers.

As author Lauren Smith Brody says, "Anyone who thought work-from-home, flex, and remote work were impossible is eating crow. It should be all on the table. The generation now and coming up the pipeline, as well as everyone going through pandemic, are considering all the variables in their lives" and will seek employers who can meet their needs for flexibility.

At some point (probably sometime between my writing the book and it being published), both my friends' employers will probably get back to some sort of new normal. Your company probably will, too. Most will likely have many of their employees come back to the office, but also retain significant elements of work-from-home.

In this chapter, we'll consider the full range of workplace flexibility options, including formal and informal approaches to time and place flexibility. Next, we'll cover criteria that can help you decide on the mix of policies and approaches that might best serve your workplace. We'll discuss implementation issues, including overcoming resistance and getting managers on board- ensuring that flexible work becomes part of the accepted organizational culture. Finally, we'll dive into the example of Flexjobs.com, a company that was founded on the principles of flexibility and has been successful working fully remotely for the past 14 years. Their example can help us consider how we can get the best out of flex and compensate for the in-person activities we miss.

Ultimately, you need to make decisions about workflex that are right for your company and enable you to express your Whole Person Workplace values. We'll start by discussing the various flavors of workplace flexibility. (One note- because these concepts overlap so much, I will use the terms remote work, workflex, telecommuting, and work-from-home mostly interchangeably in this chapter.)

WHAT'S NEXT FOR FLEX

Some employers, including leading tech companies like Twitter, Facebook and Slack, have declared that their entre workforces can work remotely for the foreseeable future[3], or even permanently[4]. Given their cultures, the type of work they do, their real-estate costs, and their ability to recruit employees nationally and internationally, this decision makes sense for them. Others will bring all their employees back together in person as soon as they can establish workplace safety. In fact, some, like Phillips 66 and Credit Agricole, recalled their "non-essential" office workforces as early as summer 2020[5].

Most employers will adopt a middle-ground approach. Some will maintain core hours but allow more discretion on whether to come in.

Others may leave it up to employees to determine when or if they need to be in the office. Others may implement four-day work weeks. As a consultant told me about her workplace, "our main office allows up to 75% capacity, but employees are free to 'return as they wish.' They've been generous with flexibility and balance for us." Many will phase in and evolve their approach over time. Some will establish explicit policies, while others will handle things informally.

Some, like my lawyer friend, have thrived working from home. Others, like my friend with two young daughters, need the office for their psychological health and to do their best work. Of course, many essential employees never went remote at all.

A one-size-fits-all approach is probably not the way to go. You should consider multiple approaches to flex, appropriate to the type of work people do as well as their personal preferences and most effective working styles. As pioneering work-life scholar Tim Hall one professed, "The most important need for many employees is not to get away from work, but to find satisfying ways to combine work and family life… What we need are less rigid forms of work flexibility[6]."

Microsoft agrees. The heart of their new policy on flexibility is simple, "Moving forward, it is our goal to offer as much flexibility as possible to support individual work styles, while balancing business needs and ensuring we live our culture[7]." As Kathleen Hogan, Microsoft's chief people officer, correctly points out, "Flexibility can mean different things to each of us, and we recognize there is no one-size-fits-all solution given the variety of roles, work requirements, and business needs we have at Microsoft."

The decisions about when, whether, and how to bring employees back are quite complex. No matter where you land on the spectrum from "everyone work from anywhere" to a hybrid approach to "everybody be here in person", you'll need to examine your values, your competitive position, the type of work being done, and the needs of your employees.

Only after careful consideration will you be able to make Whole-Person Workplace decisions about workplace flexibility.

APPROACHES TO TIME FLEXIBILITY

Flextime

With flextime, employees come to the workplace for the typical amount of hours, but can shift their work times earlier or later than the usual "9 to 5." For example, some can work "7 to 3", so they can be home for their kids after school, and others may prefer "10:30-6:30." Flextime enables employees to arrange their work schedules around caregiving or other demands. Most companies that provide flextime mandate core days and hours in which all employees must be at the workplace, for example, Mondays through Thursdays from 10am to 2pm.

Compressed Work Weeks

One particularly effective form of flextime is the compressed work week (CWW). This involves working longer hours each work day, but then earning days off. The most common CWWs include a 4-10 plan (four 10-hour days per week) or, 9-9 plan (nine 9-hour days in a two-week period).

From the employer's point of view, CWWs assure full-time hours and make scheduling more predictable. They can also be offered not just to white-collar employees, but can be extended to all facets of your workplace- for example, you can still maintain adequate shift coverage in your warehouse by staggering the "tenth day" that employees using a 9-9 plan have off. As such, CWW are a good way to provide flexibility for all and for many kinds of work.

For employees, CWWs can allow for long weekends and time off during normal working days and times. This makes it far easier for employees to make doctor's appointments, run errands, or arrange for the electrician without having to dip into PTO or wait until less convenient evenings or weekends. CWWs reduce the need for paid childcare and commuting expenses. As one happy federal employee on a 9-9 plan explains[8]:

I love my schedule. I work a little longer each day, but then get every other Friday off. We usually take advantage of this by driving up to my in-laws on Thursday night. Then, my pre-school aged kids get grandparent time and my wife and I can sleep in, relax and have some couple time. If we don't drive up to the in-laws, we sometimes use that Friday to see a movie or go to the children's museum when these things aren't so crowded.

Informal Flex

Many employers have experienced an informal sort of flextime during the pandemic. As Danielle DeBoer, a Global Business HR Partner at Novartis describes, "Employers have had to understand and be flexible. It's been ok if an employee works 8-10am, helps their kid with second grade, comes back at 1, and then works in and out through the evening."

Part-Time Scheduling

Finally, part-time scheduling and job sharing are other options. Job-sharing is an arrangement in which two employees shift to part time and collaboratively share one full-time role. While job sharing has advantages[9], few employers offer and even fewer employees utilize job sharing[10].

Reduced work scheduling, in which a full-time employee steps down to part-time during a challenging time in their lives (or when coming back from parental leave) is more common. However, this arrangement is often problematic. Too many professionals who opt for temporary part-time assignments end up working close to their usual full-time hours-due to social pressure, work demands, internal competition, and unclear boundaries. This defeats the very purpose of the arrangement.

A friend of mine who worked for a "Big 4" global financial firm when her children were quite young opted for a part-time arrangement due to high work-family demands. As she told me:

We agreed to reduce my work hours to 25 a week, with a matching reduction in salary- although I kept my benefits and seniority and the like. However, with such a work-first mindset at my job, I found that after just a few weeks, I felt the need to work very close to my original full-time hours, but was just making less money.

She returned to full-time work for a while, and then found employment elsewhere not long after that. A more far-sighted Whole-Person Workplace probably wouldn't have lost her.

In an effort to avoid some of these predictable problems with reduced work schedules, Amazon created technical units in which everyone- employees and supervisors- works 30 hours a week at 75% of typical pay and full benefits[11]. Having intact units work the same reduced schedule seems to be a smarter strategy than having a few 30-hour employees mixed in with more-than-full-time employees.

APPROACHES TO PLACE FLEXIBILITY- REMOTE WORK, TELECOMMUTING, AND WORK FROM HOME

Most often, telecommuting means working from home using computers, smartphones, and internet connections, although co-working facilities, satellite offices, and even hotel rooms[12] are sometimes used as alternate places to work.

Some employers embrace full-time remote work, in which employees work entirely from home and rarely if ever enter the traditional workplace. In just a few pages, we'll consider how Flexjobs.com runs a successful operation with a fully distributed, fully remote workforce. However, if you are considering this approach, you need to revisit how you manage employees, including your approach to hiring, evaluating performance, and ensuring sufficient collaboration. You don't want remote employees to be "out of sight, out of mind"- getting lost in the shuffle when it comes to promotions and career advancement. You need to assure enough communication to foster collaboration, creativity, and workplace culture. Remote employees can feel isolated, so we also need to tend to their emotional wellness and need for connection.

Others embrace a part-time or hybrid telecommuting model, in which employees work at the office some days and work from home on others, following an agreed-upon schedule. For example, an employee may work from home on Tuesdays and Fridays. Designating one or two days a week when everyone is available at the workplace makes it easier to schedule meetings and group work. However, if you plan to downsize your office space or real estate footprint, hybrid telecommuting can help you restrict the number of employees you have on campus on any given day.

Finally, some employers emphasize ad-hoc telecommuting in which employees, usually in consultation with supervisors, coworkers, and clients, decide which days to be in the office and which days are better spent working remotely. As-needed telecommuting empowers employees to create customized solutions that work for them, while avoiding locking into formal policies. As Tim Hall observed in the above quote, "less rigid forms of flexibility" are often the best solution. Bill Plastine at BASF agrees:

> *Designing policies that are highly flexible can engender a culture of flexibility and agility in workplace. The BASF of the past used to have 37-point plans and binders of policy manuals and procedures for everything. Increasingly, we are designing policies with simplicity in mind. For example, moving towards a two-page flex policy that more closely represents a set of guidelines, rather than over-proscribing the exact details. This gives people a more flexible culture and better ways to customize what works for them in their context.*

In short, employees are able to make the most productive use of their working hours when they can adjust the time and place of their work to avoid conflicts with other responsibilities[13]. Informal and ad-hoc arrangements often prove to be more effective than formal flex programs.

Allowing employees to construct working arrangements that suit the content of their jobs, their working styles, and their family and other non-work demands- while upholding performance standards- can be a great solution for everyone.

There are obvious advantages of remote work for employees, including reduced commuting, increased work autonomy, and an increased ability to integrate work and family demands on customized schedule. Employers also benefit by reducing office space requirements and costs; increasing employee retention, especially those who need support for their life challenges; and attracting and considering talent from beyond their local labor market. Perhaps most importantly, creating more flexible approaches to where and when work gets done allows employers to express their Whole-Person Workplace values.

I strongly recommend that all employers, even those who want their "non-essential" employees working at the office, build a policy for ad-hoc flexibility. This will be useful in the case of family emergencies, adverse weather events, or when the next big disruption occurs.

For example, many years ago, before telecommuting was on the radar for most companies, Herb Greenberg, the founder of Caliper, a leading HR and analytics consultancy, advocated for workplace flexibility. He explained, "because we had embraced telecommuting before all of our competitors, we were able to keep working even after a major snow storm. That storm resulted in one of our most profitable days ever[14]."

Some companies, including a few profiled later in the book, have transformed themselves through flexibility. Such thorough transformation can seem too intimidating to implement. By contrast, developing a capacity for informal measures of flexibility enables you to start small and then expand your approach at a more measured pace. Flexibility can be a gradual process, the first steps of which can take many different forms[15]. Flexibility doesn't have to be all or nothing. In fact, it's usually better when it's not.

CONSIDERATIONS FOR YOUR WHOLE-PERSON APPROACH TO FLEX

There are several critical factors to consider as you decide on your approach to flexibility[16].

Redesigning Work and Workflow to Enable Flexibility

Not all jobs are conducive to time or place flexibility- as the distinction between essential and non-essential employees during the height of Covid made clear. However, most jobs, and certainly most white-collar jobs, have certain duties that are amenable to being done at alternate times or at places other than the office. If you look at the jobs you supervise and break them into their component parts, it is likely you'll find that many tasks lend themselves to time and place flexibility.

A marketing research specialist, for example, needs to collaborate with colleagues and clients. However, she also has tasks that are best done alone and undistracted. Someone in this job may be a good candidate for part-time telecommuting, perhaps one or two days from home. In this way, the specialist has uninterrupted time for deep study and analysis, without the distractions of the office (and saving time and money on a commute), while also being present enough of the workweek for collaboration, conversations, and creativity. Or, perhaps owing to a positive remote working experience through 2020, this employee can be entrusted with an as-needed approach to where she works.

In her groundbreaking research[17], economist Claudia Goldin found that those in careers in which work is substitutable are freer to work more flexibly because task completion is not dependent on an individual employee. You may be able to increase substitutability in a few ways.

First, you can increase the use of teamwork by distributing responsibility for a project or client to a small team rather than a single individual. When multiple employees can share responsibility, you always have someone available for that client even if someone else is working remotely or is temporarily out of touch. A team-based approach means that work can be completed and emergencies can be addressed without every member being present or on-call 24/7, enabling employees to put down the smartphone while at home, on weekends, on vacation, or parental leave, knowing that teammates can fill in seamlessly.

You can generate similar benefits by pairing senior and junior employees on projects or client accounts. The junior staffer gains experience and exposure by working with someone more expert; the senior staffer can delegate tasks, freeing up time; the organization develops talent. This arrangement also means that, at times, the protégé can step in, reducing the need for the mentor to be constantly present or on-call.

For example, a few years ago at my university, we changed from paper forms to online student evaluations of classroom teaching. At first, only the leader of our technology team knew the system well enough to troubleshoot problems- which made her life very difficult and caused a bottleneck of unresolved issues. Once she was able to get multiple members of her team fully oriented, the team distributed troubleshooting duties, making everyone's lives easier while providing better internal customer service. She could even take a day off every now and then without bringing work to a screeching halt.

Careful reconsideration of job design and workflow can uncover opportunities for flexible work. State Street Bank has been highly successful implementing this principle through their award-winning manager-initiated flex program[18], in which supervisors are responsible for uncovering and continually expanding opportunities for their employees to work flexibly.

Alternatives for When Work Can't Flex

Some work needs to be done in person at the workplace. For those performing these jobs, there is less room for flexibility. However, there are other ways we can support these employees. First, structured approaches to flextime, such as compressed work weeks, work well in environments where you need to ensure adequate shift coverage- as in a factory, warehouse, hotel, or hospital.

However, for many hourly employees, schedule certainty is the key workplace factor that allows for better work-family balance. When a waiter or a retail employee only gets a few days' notice whether they are working day or night shifts or if their schedule can be changed last-minute, it can wreak havoc on their family's schedule. How can someone make or keep a doctor's appointment or know if they can pick up their kids from day care? Scheduling time for life's challenges becomes extremely difficult. You can make an incredible difference for employees if you can be part of the solution. Whole-person Workplaces are for all employees, not just the already privileged.

Several years ago at the 2014 White House Summit for Working Families[19], Macy's employee Kay Thompson made the important distinction between the need for more flexibility for white-collar employees and for schedule certainty for blue-collar and hourly employees. She gave a moving address describing the collective bargaining agreement between Macy's and her union that guaranteed: employees get their work schedules at least three weeks in advance, they can choose days off up to six months in advance, and they can designate, ahead of time, particular days they could not be asked to come in early or stay late. "This assured stability in scheduling allows me to prepare my children for school every day.... While I am grateful for my work situation, I want all retail workers to experience a sustainable working environment where family-friendly workplace scheduling is a priority for all companies[20]."

For Tom Prendergast, co-owner of Jugtown Country Store, a small New Hampshire retailer with 12 employees, only 5 of which are full-time, constant communication and informal flexibility are paramount.

In terms of scheduling, we start with getting our employees' preferences. Things come up in life. If someone needs Tuesday night off, we'll see if someone can cover for them, or switch shifts and that usually works out. If not, and if it's not all the time, I'll pick up their shift. They support me every day, so I can support them when they need.

Our general manager has a newborn, a preschooler and a teenager, also an ill mother, and she's had some Covid scares in her extended family. We catered to her scheduling needs as best we can with a full team effort. So many employees stepped up to cover or switch shifts with her, and we tried to recognize them for it- sometimes with gift cards and discounts and such. We wanted to make sure that the fact that they sacrificed for her didn't go unnoticed. Also, because of her special circumstances, we got her a computer so she could do some of her work from home.

At New Moon Natural Foods, with two locations in the Lake Tahoe area and 90 employees, about 60% who are full-time, part of their scheduling solution is developing a cadre of key part-timers who can fill in or take extra shifts when needed- providing a buffer for when full-time employees need time off or for staffing up during busy holiday seasons.

Besides scheduling, we need to make it a point to support all of our employees, especially our "essential workers." After all, they are facing a host of new workplace safety concerns and carry the anxiety of contracting a potentially deadly disease and infecting their loved ones. If we can't offer flexibility, the least we can do is assure livable wages, solid core benefits like health insurance, retirement savings, and opportunities for education and development, Further, ensuring physically safe work environments and providing health and wellness benefits are especially important for those on the front lines, factory floors and retail aisles (We will consider these policies in more detail in Chapters 6 through 8).

Assessing the People Involved

Some employees are better candidates for flexibility than others. If you have a high-performing employee who has proven he can self-manage well, you probably can entrust him with more flexibility. If you have an unproven employee, or one whom you feel needs more structure and hands-on guidance, I'd talk to them about what they need to demonstrate before they earn a more flexible arrangement. Personality-related factors, such as introversion/extraversion and whether someone works best integrating work and life or compartmentalizing the two[21], should also be part of your consideration.

For these reasons, I recommend that ad-hoc workplace flexibility arrangements start with an initial trial period. By doing so, you can better gauge how an employee either rises to the occasion or struggles with flex and adjust accordingly. As an additional benefit, you can use conversations around job design and your level of trust in an employee as you consider the degree to which you'll provide flexible work opportunities.

Assessing Your Work Culture

The decisions you make about workplace flexibility can have a significant effect on your organizational culture. You can talk all you want about Whole-Person Workplace values, but if your policies and follow-through do not match, these become empty words. If you truly value your employees as whole people, developing an approach to flexibility is one of the most impactful ways you can express it. In fact, perhaps more than any other topic in this book, flexibility gets to the heart of the matter, as it allows employees the respect and time they need to attend to their life challenges. As Doreen Anthony, the VP of HR at Concord Health puts it, "there's no greater gift than time."

The recent experience of Johnstone Supply, a northeast-based HVAC wholesale supplier, illustrates the importance of a well-considered comprehensive, flexible approach to workplace flexibility- jobs, people, and culture- even during the height of the pandemic. According to CHRO Chris Geschickter:

Over the last six months, we probably changed protocols 5 times. It is a living document, because things keep changing- the pandemic kept changing, laws kept changing- what if schools don't re-open? But we always look to our core company values- which will not change.

We have lots of customer-facing repair and delivery people, essential employees in warehouses and retail, as well as office professionals. Every group needed a different approach. Some could telecommute, others needed to be there, but we had to do everything we could to keep employees and customers safe. As a smaller company, I know all 140 employees. I know who they are what they do, their families, their needs. And that's where we start- what works best for individuals.

IMPLEMENTING FLEX

Once you decide on a flexibility strategy (or strategies), you need to manage this process and make sure it is adequately supported.

Managing Logistics

In March 2020, Robert Russo, an executive HR director at Bristol-Myers Squibb, remembers thinking, "How are we going to provide the resources for our people to work from home long-term? Do we need to buy laptops for 35,000 employees? Why? Why not? We have to explore all ideas." His concerns underscore some of the logistical challenges to widespread remote work. After all, regardless of your Whole-Person Workplace intentions, you can't do great things for your employees if you don't execute well from an operational standpoint. Your HR, finance, and IT folks can help you figure out the best solutions for your workplace. And, of course, you'll need to talk to a wide cross-section of employees to better understand their needs.

As Sarah Sutton and Karen LaGraff of Flexjobs.com note, "If employees have a video streaming service like Netflix in their home that works ok, then they should have adequate internet capability to use Zoom or other video conferencing applications[22]." And, yes, thankfully, the costs of information technology are at a point where most employers can afford scalable solutions.

However, there are other considerations besides adequate Wi-Fi, which is far from universal. You also need to make sure everyone has the computer hardware and software they need to succeed. It used to be hard to find good options, but now the trick is sifting through the many available products and deciding what is right for you. Zoom, Microsoft Teams, Webex, or Skype for Business? Slack or Yammer? GoToMyPc? You also need to consider data security, VPNs, secure sharing, and two-factor authentication. Security is especially important with client data, considering that employees may be working on laptops in common spaces in their homes or in public areas.

Once you figure out the technical solutions, you also need to figure out who pays for what. If employees are required to work from home, their Wi-Fi, printer cartridges, and other office supplies may no longer be considered solely personal or personal business expenses. They may more appropriately be costs borne by employers. I am not a lawyer, but you might want to consult one about these issues. There are also OSHA considerations- if the home is the workplace, what are the standards for workplace safety and ergonomic work stations? Things get complicated very quickly. During the height of the pandemic, quick decisions were good enough. In the new normal, you'll have to be more considered.

Addressing Supervisory Concerns

Even after the Covid-induced work-from-home revolution, some managers may still resist remote work, especially if the pandemic recedes. Perhaps they saw flex as a necessary evil in 2020 but want to get back to a pre-Covid normal as soon as possible. Some of these resistant managers' concerns include[23]:

» Employees may abuse the privilege and slack off

» A lack of coworker interaction may harm cohesiveness, new ideas, and collective performance

» They will lose the ability to evaluate and manage employee performance without "face time"

» They personally don't like working remotely and fail to consider others' preferences

» If they allow some employees to work flexibly, others will also approach them for flex

In fact, many of these fears are unfounded or exaggerated. However, it is your job as a leader to address these concerns. If you don't, you'll get, at best, passive-aggressive compliance, but you'll never really get them on board.

I recommend starting small and expanding gradually, as this helps assure managers that nothing is falling through the cracks. HR can provide templates for progress reporting, time use logs, and other ways to document employee work. Leaders can encourage frequent goal-setting and coaching sessions in which supervisors and workers create and review clear deadlines for deliverables. Over time, as their concerns are addressed, even reluctant managers are far more likely to support flexible work.

As we'll see in later chapters, Ryan, LLC overhauled their performance evaluation system[24] in order to generate support for its shift to a results-only work environment. Instead of periodic, largely subjective supervisor evaluations supplemented by a running total of billable hours, Ryan created a continually-updated dashboard of key performance metrics. This dashboard assured skeptical managers that great work was still being done, even at unconventional times and places. Ryan's approach may be more advanced than your current capabilities, but you can start small with some of the ideas I've listed above.

Another way to help supervisors get on board is if HR or leadership can give supervisors a guide for conversations about workflex and how to handle employee requests. Brie Reynolds of Flexjobs explains:

60% of managers have total discretion about who works remotely. The criteria they use can be very confusing and engender negative reactions about remote work- special treatment, 'why not me?' When you have a transparent guide and a structured approach to decision making it helps everyone feel better about flex.

... Let me tell you about one client company of ours. ADP has a great hybrid culture. They have remote, flex, and in-office employees, and they structure this very well. No one feels uncertain about things. People know why they are in the office and know who and why others are home. No questions about why or how. They maintain consistent values and norms between these two situations, with lots of transparency.

A structured approach reduces anxiety around requests for flex and ameliorates hard feelings if requests aren't fully approved.

Addressing Remote Worker Concerns- "Out of Sight, Out of Mind"

A major concern of employees who flex, especially when others aren't, is that they can feel "out of sight, out of mind." That is, because they are not physically present, supervisors and coworkers may ignore their contributions, fail to include them in opportunities, or improperly value their work.

Relatedly, many feel socially isolated and miss the personal connections they have at work. Beth Rivera of Uncommon Goods describes the situation well. There are many social reasons that remote working may not be equally embraced by everyone:

Many people enjoy the remote work but really miss their colleagues. For some, home is overwhelming- husband and kids and dogs and school and all. For others who live alone, remote work can be very isolating. Others aren't comfortable on video or in their physical location- do I want people to see me on my bed in a studio apartment, when others have the whole impressive bookshelf home office?

To address these concerns, you need to ensure that remote workers have sufficient interaction with the rest of the workplace. We should ensure supervisors have regular "check-in" meetings with their employees to discuss work and career opportunities, assuring remote employees that they are out of neither sight nor mind. Have enough Zoom work meetings and plan online social events. Sutton and LaGraff cheerily recommend, "Don't forget to have fun! Online video meetings don't have to be just for work; they can also be to have coffee breaks, celebrate birthdays or holidays, or even host a virtual happy hour to build camaraderie.[25]"

Even at a distance, we can find little fun moments to build connection. At my university, for example, we couldn't celebrate with our May 2020 graduates in person. Instead, my academic unit held a pizza party- students joined us in a big Zoom meeting, and we surprised them by delivering a pizza to all of their houses all at the same time. It was a big hit and an appreciated gesture during a difficult time.

Addressing Remote Worker Concerns- Work-Life Overlap

Another concern is the tendency for work-from-home to obliterate work-life separation. Jessica DeGroot of Thirdpath Institute has often cautioned that "flexible workplaces may be great, but they sometimes do a poor job with human capacity management." That is, people are allowed to work flexibly- as long as they do much more work. If you can work from anywhere and anytime, well, you can keep working from anywhere and anytime. Sometimes, even in the absence of outside pressure to do so, we get glued to our laptops and smartphones and add this extra burden to ourselves. Danielle DeBoer of Novartis explains:

Work-life balance or separation? For a lot of us, it feels like with remote work there's more work and more meetings than ever before. Some research shows people are working more hours, and will this now be the expectation? It's a weird place we're all in. What will happen in the new normal? Back in the office, is it 40 or 50 again, or just 30 if you get everything done?

Robert Russo of Bristol-Myers Squibb reports that, during 2020, a lot of employees put off taking vacation, "There wasn't anywhere they could go." He was happy that BMS was encouraging people to take time off, even if they didn't leave their house (which, of course was now also their workplace). They even had a company-wide day off as a mental health break.

Employers need to encourage remote workers to adhere to regular schedules, take frequent breaks, and make use of their PTO. Failure to do so risks chronic overwork, and all of the negative physical and mental health consequences that go along with it. Chronic overwork, as we'll discuss in Chapter 6, is a leading cause of burnout and turnover.

Further, managers and leaders can role-model flexible work. If your employees see you occasionally shifting hours or using technology to work at a distance, they will feel more comfortable doing the same. Finally, leaders should take great care to mentor proper capacity management. If a team sees their boss emailing them at 11 at night or on the weekends, they'll feel the pressure to be constantly plugged in. When it comes to Whole-Person Workplace values, we have to walk the talk.

LESSONS FROM A LONG-STANDING REMOTE WORKPLACE

To conclude this chapter, I'm going to turn the floor over to Brie Reynolds, the career development manager at Flexjobs.com, a leading employment service for remote and flexible work. They have been a fully-remote distributed workplace since their founding. Reynolds discusses how Flexjobs has thrived with remote work.

We were founded as a remote company in 2007. It's always been top of mind. How do we grow and develop our culture- create a productive, collaborative workplace with shared values and social connections? Not just do our work and get it done- but be part of something bigger.

We try to do this in ways large and small, trying to be thoughtful and intentional. We made remote work part of our culture. Our senior level people all see this as important. Not just our founder and CEO, but everyone leading teams understands our culture around flex.

When we think of culture-building activities, we think about how would it have been done in an office, then how can we do this remotely and still have it be fun. Things like office parties, baby showers, our annual Halloween party. These things are all common in an office. So how do we translate this into a remote environment?

We all wore costumes on our zoom calls before Halloween- 'I have a question for the werewolf!' We all pitched in for a collective present for an online baby shower, so she'd have something to open. We have pizza parties- we all ordered our favorite pizza to be delivered at the same time and then just had fun together. It takes just a little extra thought and effort for these things to happen. And then, you can learn things about your colleagues, and build your community and culture.

... In terms of orienting new hires in this environment, we recently brought five on board. One of them said our onboarding process was better than any in-person orientation they experienced before. At his last company, he wasn't onboarded at all, just brought to his cubicle, and 'oh, right... we forgot to order you a computer.' How is an employee going to make sure they deal with all the details if the company doesn't?

It helps a new employee so much if you can give structure to their initial days, make them feel part of real team, and see how everything works together. We set up individual meeting times for them to learn about the whole company. For the first two weeks, they spend about 2-3 hours a day meeting with teammates and attending trainings. We set up follow-up check-in times so we can really show them what their worklife will be like.

... Open communication is foundational. How well do managers communicate with employees and how well does the senior level communicate with workforce? We have "quarantine check-in templates" to facilitate this. It's basically a progress report, but not just what you accomplished, but also explaining how work-life is colliding, what is good, what is a struggle, how this affects you and your schedule going forward. This template leads to a 15-minute conversation with your manager and can make a big difference.

THE FINAL WORD

By allowing workers more control over when and where they work, we can help them achieve the balance they need to rise to their family and life challenges. In the short-term, this maintains and even enhances their job performance. In the long-term, it attracts and retains top talent- the kinds of professionals who do their best work when they know they are trusted and valued as whole people with full lives. Even if they sometimes get dressed up like werewolves.

THOUGHTS AND ADVICE

» Remote work, in some form, is here to stay. Employers need to consider their options and craft whole-person policies to support employees.

» Options range from full-time remote work, to hybrid and ad-hoc approaches. Each have advantages and disadvantages and are more appropriate under certain conditions.

» Creating customized, as-needed and informal solutions can be especially effective.

» Your flexibility mix should be based in part on the work to be done and the employees involved. You should consider redesigning workflow to enable additional flexibility.

» Recognize that some workers can't work flexibly, but we can support them in other ways, including respecting their non-work time with schedule certainly.

» The logistics involved in work-from-home should not be underestimated. Hardware, software, connectivity, data security, and legal issues all need to be considered.

» Supervisors need to be engaged in workflex, and efforts must be made to overcome the reasons some supervisors may resist.

» Remote workers can feel socially isolated and disconnected from peers. There are ways to recreate the social side of work, even at a distance.

» Flexjobs.com has operated successfully as an all-remote workplace for 14 years and, through consistent effort, have built a tight-knit work culture.

CHAPTER 3 – MAKING PARENTAL LEAVE WORK FOR EVERYONE

EMPLOYEES HAVE BABIES. For new parents, this is life-changing. For employers, however, someone having a baby and taking parental leave shouldn't be a seismic event.

If you employ enough people, some of them will have children (in any given year about 4.7% of women of child bearing age become pregnant[1], and most of them have partners, so about 8% of your age 20 to mid-40s workforce may need parental leave in a given year). As I see it, too many employers fail to plan. They end up treating each instance of an employee having a child as an unexpected one-off situation. "OMG, how are we going to manage over the next month without Carol?" Happily, there are many ways you can help your workplace thrive during these situations, embed parental leave into your everyday work processes, and even leverage these situations into developmental opportunities.

By supporting new parents, especially mothers, with parental leave and other early-childhood supports at a time in which they need significant help, you build a Whole-Person Workplace. The year after childbirth is an especially high-risk time for turnover[2]- a well-crafted parental leave policy can have a huge impact on retention. For example, when Accenture doubled leave from eight weeks to 16, its turnover rate for new mothers fell by 40%[3].

In an era in which gender equity and the need for diverse leadership teams are more crucial than ever, it becomes even more important to retain women. As author Lauren Smith Brody attests, "When you support new mothers during the crucible of their first year, you'll eventually have more women growing into leadership roles, resulting in better led, more diverse and more highly motivated leadership teams. This directly relates to long-term financial success."

The benefits of well-crafted parental leave do not extend only to new mothers. Consider the different experiences of these two fathers I interviewed for my previous book, *The Working Dad's Survival Guide*[4]:

> *I have to say, my employer was wonderful with the birth of my daughter. I had paid leave for 4 weeks and used my vacation for an additional 2 weeks. It's one of the reasons why I turned down another job that offered me more money.*
>
> -
>
> *My daughter was in the NICU for 22 days. I was allowed to work from the hospital for a few weeks, then told I had to come into the office at least three days a week. I was told I was 'like a kid in high school smoking the restroom' and they were covering for me. Even though my job could be done from anywhere, they wouldn't let me work remotely. I quit a few days later.*

Two new dads. One valued as a whole person, one not. One who remained with his employer- grateful for the support and happy to reciprocate. The other, burned out and now adding value at a different, hopefully more supportive employer.

In this chapter, we'll discuss how to craft parental leave policies that assist new parents while respecting coworkers and ensuring continuity of performance. We'll discuss many overlooked aspects of a successful leave policy, including managing workflow, communication strategy, approaches to gradual re-entry, rethinking compensation and career progression, and the need to include both moms and dads. With these applicable lessons, you can be confident that your approach to parental leave will work for everyone involved.

EIGHT BABIES A DAY

Teresa McDade, the Director of Work-Life Benefits at Microsoft, explains the need for a comprehensive parental leave policy:

We were having 8 babies a day and were still managing each situation individually. It became untenable.[5]

That's over 2,900 babies a year! If leaves are to be this frequent, there should be a more comprehensive approach. Thanks to McDade and her team, parental leave success at Microsoft starts with a robust policy (they provide 20 weeks for birth moms, 12 weeks for others[6]). Microsoft also built support structures around leave, so that employees can use the policy with confidence. Their leave program involves conversations and planning sessions with supervisors and coworkers, ensuring that quality work continues to get done and non-parents don't feel over-burdened. This means parental leave works for everyone- reducing resistance and fostering a Whole-Person culture.

I met McDade through my friend, Amy Beacom, who, at the time, was using her passion and expertise as a parental leave consultant to help employees get the most out of Microsoft's policy.

Beacom's passion for parental leave consulting was energized by her difficult experience during what should have been one of the happiest times of her life. She was working on her dissertation at a prestigious university and having her first child. Instead, that year was harder than it needed to be. Feeling unsupported by her university during her pregnancy, childbirth, and recovery, and while fighting post-partum depression, her mind focused on one thought, which has sustained her work ever since:

I never want anyone else to feel as alone as I do right now.

That time in her life was so hard because, at her university (where, as a doctoral candidate, she was both employee and student), there was no allowance for family concerns, no accommodation for her situation. "It was horrible, and it could have been done differently." She had worked for great employers before and, in her prior career in executive development, seen first-hand how supervisory support leads to personal and business success.

For her dissertation, Beacom designed an evidence-based coaching program to prepare expectant mothers to transition to their new life-long role of working parent, with an emphasis on using parental leave as a developmental opportunity. This program serves as the foundation of her consultancy, the Center for Parental Leave Leadership (CPLL)- the first to focus specifically on parental leave coaching.

Fast-forward a few years to when CPLL partnered with McDade and with Wellspring EAP to provide web-based coaching for expectant parents at Microsoft. Their training was successful, but they correctly surmised that the training sessions for new fathers would be more accessible if they were led by a man, especially one who specialized in fathers' work-family issues.

So, Beacom called me to be the "dad trainer." Using her model, with a few important tweaks for men, I helped expectant fathers at Microsoft plan for their leaves, feel more confident as new dads, and return to work with a better understanding of the joys and stressors of being a working parent.

This project was also my education on what makes for successful parental leave. Great policy, crafted by HR experts, supported by top leadership, and complemented with a host of measures to ensure that it works well for everyone. Here are some of the lessons I learned and examples from other employers who have made it work. But first, here's the current state of parental leave in the United States.

PARENTAL LEAVE IN THE USA

The current situation of parental leave in the USA doesn't work for employees or employers. We are the only industrialized country in the world without mandated paid maternity leave[7] and are in a distinct minority of countries without paid paternity leave[8]. When you compare national parental leave policies, they range from zero paid weeks (the USA) to 86 (Estonia)[9]. When you combine paid and unpaid leave, as well as leave given to both members of a couple, some countries offer over two years.

Author Lauren Smith Brody captures the frustration with this situation perfectly, "Even Japan- a country that employs people with sticks to smush commuters onto the crowded subways to get to work on time- grants mothers 14 weeks at 60% pay.[10]" Instead, we have a federal unpaid leave program, several state paid leave programs, and wide variety in whether and how private employers offer paid parental leave.

As a result, employees in the US are more dependent on their employers for family leave than in any other country on Earth. As Julia Beck of the It's Working Project notes, "You shouldn't have had to win the boss lottery to get maternity leave." Unfortunately, according to a recent World at Work survey, only about 38% of private employers offer paid parental leave, and their average length of leave was 4.1 weeks[11].

The USA's unpaid leave program, the Family and Medical Leave Act, provides up to 12 unpaid weeks of leave to new parents- but eligibility is subject to so many conditions that its benefits extend to only 60% or so of the US workforce[12]. You have to have worked long enough, at a near full-time capacity, for an employer with at least 50 employees- among other specifications. Freelancers, the self-employed, those cobbling together part-time work, and those working for smaller employers are out of luck. And even when people are eligible, only a privileged slice of the workforce can afford to be without pay for up to 12 weeks.

Currently, five US states and Washington DC have implemented paid family leave programs[13]. Four more states have approved programs that are not yet up and running. In general, these policies are funded through a small payroll tax into a state-run family leave insurance program, which then provides partial wage replacement (usually up to 2/3 salary, up to a maximum) for six to twelve weeks. Employers do not have to pay employees during leave, but they need to maintain benefits, are obligated to preserve the leave-taker's position, and cannot retaliate.

This patchwork solution creates a real problem for employers. Those in states with paid leave policies often feel over-regulated and at a competitive disadvantage to companies operating elsewhere- even when employers don't absorb the direct costs associated with leave, they incur indirect costs such as overtime and temporary help. Those that operate in multiple states must balance disparate policies (those that operate internationally have an even bigger problem).

As Dave Bolotsky, CEO of Uncommon Goods, told me, "Employers need to go beyond minimum public policy if they are going to value employees as whole people." As a result, many employers develop their own paid leave policies, ranging from a week or two at reduced pay, to upwards of 16 weeks fully paid.

Overall, this situation is confusing for managers and stressful for expectant parents. Unsupported new parents, especially mothers, are a huge turnover risk, but too many employers have yet to articulate and follow-through with robust Whole-Person leave policies.

CRAFTING AN EFFECTIVE WHOLE-PERSON PARENTAL LEAVE POLICY

Length of Leave

The most basic element of crafting an effective parental leave policy is determining how long the leave should be. You want to support new parents while balancing the needs of the business and those still at the workplace. The length of leave should vary on a number of factors.

» How does parental leave reflect my values as an employer?

» What do my competitors offer?

» How much can I afford, knowing I may need to hire temporary help?

» What is the makeup of my workforce? (age, gender, other demographics)

» What do my employees want?

So, what is the right amount of time for your company? In part, the answer depends on your values.

Online wholesale retailer Boxed offers unlimited paid parental leave. That's right, unlimited. New parents decide for themselves how much time they will take. Founder and CEO Chieh Huang says it's important that employees come back when they are ready[14]:

When you look at the data over the last almost four years that we've been doing this, it's worked well. The longest parental leave someone ever took was about five months. The shortest was two weeks... First time parents might think, 'Ok, I'll be back in three weeks,' but when you see your baby's face you're like, 'Alright, I'm never coming back to work.' Or there's the opposite end when you're just like, 'I'm gonna take six months,' and during the fifth week of getting an hour's night sleep you're like, 'I am definitely needing to deal with adults rather than babies.'

In part, the answer depends on your circumstances.

A few years ago, I spoke at the O.Berk Family Business Forum about what employers can do to help employees with work-life balance. Most of the audience represented small, family-owned businesses in north and central New Jersey. When I started discussing parental leave, one attendee stated that while he would like to provide his employees with extended leave, he only has two accountants, and "if one of them is out for three months, that puts a major crimp in my operations." We had an interesting discussion about this, and for this man's company, extended parental leave was not the best way to express his Whole-Person values. We discussed other supports, including flexible scheduling and work-from-home, that were more appropriate for his company.

By contrast, generous extended parental leaves make a whole lot of sense for the Microsofts of the world. When you are a successful multinational with plentiful resources and are engaged in a "war for talent" with a defined set of competitors who also offer extended programs, generous policies are a way to compete for the best talent. This is especially true when your potential employees are just a click away from Glassdoor.com, FairyGodBoss.com, Fortune's employer rankings, or other rich sources of information about how well you live up to Whole-Person Workforce ideals.

Splitting the difference may be most appropriate for most employers. For example, Uncommon Goods, a mid-sized online retailer with a workforce consisting of techies, white-collar types, and warehouse employees, provides 8 fully paid weeks of parental leave to all of its employees, who can then also utilize New York State's family leave benefits. Leadership at Uncommon Goods believes so strongly in valuing employees as whole people, especially supporting new parents, that they became involved in the Time to Care NY campaign that successfully lobbied for New York State's parental leave program.

Parental leave absolutely has costs. Employers are paying for time not worked and paying for ways to ensure the work continues to get done. However, we also need to consider the benefits. The costs associated with turnover are high, especially for smaller businesses, and the reputational advantages in terms of attracting, retaining, and engaging employees are real, even if they are harder to quantify.

In the final analysis, and considering the intangible cultural benefits, I'd work to figure out what makes the most financial sense for you, and then add a bit more time. If that extra time helps you attract or retain even one great employee, the small extra up-front investment will have paid off.

Widening the Range of Who Is Eligible

The next major decision is determining who is eligible for parental leave. Many employers require employees to work for 6 or 12 months before becoming eligible. Tenure requirements seem unnecessary; are applicants nefariously hiding pregnancies to scam employers? However, I do understand employers have an interest in ensuring employees work for them for a period of time before any sort of extended leave- whether this be parental leave, vacation time, or other PTO.

Some employers provide parental leave only to its salaried employees, and sometimes even only to those at certain levels of the company. Others have dual policies, usually with the already privileged usually getting the better deal. These decisions strike me as unfair and inconsistent with Whole-Person principles. Please consider your entire workforce as you create your policy.

There's yet another aspect to eligibility. Federal, state, and most (but not all) employer leave plans include both mothers and fathers, and birth parents as well as adoptive and foster parents[15]. This is good, as it recognizes that there are many ways to become a family, and that all parents- moms and dads- are important. After all, as Thirdpath Institute founder, Jessica DeGroot, states:

> Positive workplace changes can't happen unless you include men in solutions. Even if it's a good policy, if it is seen as just a women's issue, it won't be accepted, implemented or supported as well. We need to include men and make things like leave and flex feel safe for men to use.

I agree, and in fact, have written an entire book on this subject[16]!

It is true, however, that birth mothers have the toughest go of it- they are the ones experiencing pregnancy and childbirth. As a result, many employers understandably give birth mothers longer parental leaves (and, in fact, parental leave was initially implemented to allow new mothers time to physically recover from giving birth).

Determining leave length for different constituencies can become complicated. After several high-profile lawsuits by fathers[17], the EEOC issued guidelines concerning parental leave parity between men and women:

> *Parental leave must be provided to similarly situated men and women on the same terms. If, for example, an employer extends leave to new mothers beyond the period of recuperation from childbirth (e.g. to provide the mothers time to bond with and/or care for the baby), it cannot lawfully fail to provide an equivalent amount of leave to new fathers for the same purpose[18].*

A lot of the time, parental leave policies actually consist of two types of leave: time for physical recovery and time for care and bonding. The guideline makes it clear that dads are legally entitled to the same leave offered to new moms, excepting leave specifically for physical recovery. This means that a company that offers birth moms 8 weeks of paid leave (2 for recovery and 6 for care/bonding) should offer dads 6 weeks. The same logic extends to adoptive and foster parents. Birth moms deserve extra time for recovery, but we recognize all types of parents as whole people when they are included in our parental leave policies.

Relatedly, some employers offer a longer leave to "primary parents" and a shorter leave to "secondary caregivers," a distinction that irks me. While the practical effect is similar to providing longer leaves for birth mothers, the primary/secondary distinction seems to imply that fathers are secondary parents. This assumption, if it ever was true, certainly isn't today- and fails to validate dads as whole persons.

Communication and Logistics

One of the recurring themes of this book is that you can't do great things for your employees if you don't execute well from an operational standpoint. Amy Beacom contends this is especially true for parental leave:

It doesn't matter what kind of leave policy you have if you if your procedural elements are screwed up. You need to have a clear policy that is well communicated to employees. Your staff needs to be able to answer questions and help them navigate- 'what about my insurance?'- you need to have the answer for that. Do you have eligibility forms to fill out? Are they accessible, do managers know about them? The procedural pieces can derail an entire experience. Any company needs to start there.

Once you craft a policy, it needs to be effectively communicated- not just to your employees, but also to managers and supervisors. Managers need to be able to answer basic questions about eligibility, timeframes, and benefits- or at least need to be able to refer employees to the right person in HR. After all, an employee may make use of parental leave only once or twice in their lives, but companies may have 8 babies a day.

Communicating policy is not as simple as posting on a website or on the HR department's bulletin board. A robust and creative approach is needed to ensure everyone is aware of, and feels supported in making use of, these policies. Creating a comprehensive web portal and partnering with an employee assistance program provider with experience in these matters are great places to start. Further, think about where your employees congregate and get their information. Do employees discard emails from HR but often eat lunch together? If so, go to the lunchroom to have conversations and give out flyers. Do you have an employee gym that gets a lot of early morning use? Who are your more social and influential employees, and how can you get them to help spread the word?

Framing our communication about Whole-Person policies is also quite important. The more inclusive we can make our messaging, the better. If we talk only about maternity leave instead of parental leave, for example, we exclude fathers[19]. If we only gush over new parents, we exclude non-parents or those with older children, perpetuating a mindset that some employees are neglected while others are privileged (more on this in Chapter 5).

I recommend framing parental leave as one important part of your larger Whole-Person approach. After all, parental leave is just one form of PTO- which also includes vacation days, sick days, personal days, and time for volunteering. Even more importantly, and assuming we've created them, if we communicate the full range of ways we support employees-financial assistance, employee wellness initiatives, time for caregiving for children and elder parents, educational programs, workplace safety- then parental leave represents just one important slice of a whole. This holistic approach has the added benefit of reducing possible tension between parents and non-parents.

There are several other logistical issues many employers don't initially consider. For example, does the use of parental leave affect performance evaluations, raises, and bonuses? Amy Beacom recalls seeing "policies where people who took an extended parental leave became ineligible for that year's profit-sharing program. It dissuaded them from taking the leave they were eligible for." Lauren Smith Brody works with many law firms on their parental leave programs and observes that:

> *With a billable hours model for compensation, you can't ignore that its harder to hit target hours when you've taken leave. It's one of the reasons for the precipitous falloff of female lawyers- half of all associates are women, but only 12% of partners. I'm sure how leave is handled at many law firms plays a big role in this.*

On the one hand, the employee is missing up to several weeks of work. On the other hand, if we value employees as whole people, we shouldn't penalize them for caring for their families. On the third hand, is this fair for employees who didn't take leave? These can be tricky issues.

Wherever you end up with these decisions, my advice is to lead with a Whole-Person mindset. Of course we shouldn't penalize new parents. We also need to provide enough support for non-parents, so they feel validated and, as a result, are far less attuned to small perceived inequities.

Planning Ahead and Integrating Employee Development

In the vast majority of cases, we have months to prepare for an employee's parental leave. We should use this time wisely to make sure: (a) the employee is oriented to new parenthood and their new role of working parent, (b) coworkers and supervisors can continue to provide quality work without being over-burdened, and (c) the company and customers benefit from continuity of service.

This planning should be driven by the employee-manager partnership. HR can play a key supporting role by providing supervisory training and help in structuring initial conversations. During the planning process, it is important to involve and address the concerns of the leave-taker's coworkers. We need to ensure that the work gets done, but we don't want to overburden anyone. After all, coworkers are whole persons too. As leading work-life scholar, Alyssa Westring, details:

In our care for new parents, we sometimes overlook others. Leave doesn't just impact the worker having a baby, but also their teammates and colleagues. If we don't manage the repercussions for them, they'll wind up frustrated, feeling like things are unfair, that they are not given the same opportunities, and that they have to do extra work. How you manage the rest of the work team is very important.

CPLL's approach to parental leave coaching includes employee communication with supervisors, coworkers, and clients- ensuring that everyone is on the same page. In some cases, this means the supervisor should start looking for a temp to fill in. Sometimes, this means distributing work within your team. In other circumstances, this means using the month before leave to mentor a junior employee, so she can pick up additional responsibilities. This last option has the added benefit of both ensuring continuity of work and developing employees.

Bill Plastine, Head of Employee Development and Performance at BASF, provides an example of this win-win approach:

In some of our smaller locations, say a plant with 20 people in highly-specialized jobs, it can be a challenge to fill in during a leave. We try our best to pre-plan, but can't always. That's where lead time and open communication really helps. Sometimes we need to get a contract employee or temporary fill-in. But I think it's best when we can create a development opportunity for folks. Say in procurement- we can coach someone up so they can transition for those two months in a new assignment. This helps them build a new skillset so they can move up later on.

The employee, supervisor, and work team need to collaborate on their custom solution, considering everyone's concerns and the needs of the business. However, a sole reliance on individualized solutions does not scale; recall McDade's quote, "We were having 8 babies a day and were still managing each situation individually. It became untenable." Instead, Whole-Person employers understand that parental leave is a normal occurrence and build flexibility into their normal work operations.

BASF's Bill Plastine explains how the way his department operates makes parental leave easier for everyone:

The type of work we do is very collaborative and mostly involves long-term projects. We build teams in a way so people can jump in and out as needed. We always had enough people knowledgeable about a project to keep it running well. And those who take leave can easily pick up where we leave off. We also cross-train between projects, so we have flexibility. For example, for our onboarding program, there's not just one person involved. There's someone who owns it, but many well-versed in it so we can work as an interconnected team. I think this is a smart approach to work design that existed before leave policies, but this approach and culture works really well for these situations.

This quote emphasizes the importance of building flexibility and overlapping responsibility into regular workflow. More flexible workplaces enable employees to take leave with confidence, while insulating their colleagues from feeling overworked. This thoughtful approach to job design is also conducive to effective employee development, succession planning, and knowledge management programs.

To illustrate, not long ago, I spoke on a parental leave panel sponsored by the Employers Association of New Jersey. There, a skeptical attendee asked, "How am I supposed to make it work for 6 weeks down one or two of my 25 employees?" While I sympathized with his dilemma, I challenged his thought process. I replied, "Well, what would you do if you had two people sick, or two on vacation, or if two people quit? Are there ways you can cross-train, share responsibilities, have a temp agency at the ready? At least with parental leave, you have a few months to plan-maybe you can use that time to groom an employee to fill in?" He wasn't thrilled by my answer but admitted I gave him some ideas to consider in terms of building more resiliency into his approach.

Finally, it is straightforward to consider how having a junior employee step up during a colleague's leave can be a developmental opportunity. However, parental leaves can also create other, less obvious opportunities for development. First, many supervisors and leaders- especially older men who may not have had to directly confront work-family challenges in their own lives- may not have fully considered the challenges faced by today's working parents. The conversations they have with the employees while planning for a smooth parental leave transition can develop their empathy, awareness, and effectiveness around these issues. Further, parental leave can be a developmental opportunity for the new parents themselves. The foundation of Amy Beacom's work at CPLL is helping expectant parents consider their roles as workers, parents, and working parents; better understand their shifting priorities; and develop specific skills as delegation, boundary-setting, multi-tasking, and prioritization.

Planning for a Seamless Return from Parental Leave

New parents cherish parental leave as a precious time to bond with and care for their newborn. However, most working parents, especially those with career aspirations, don't want to fully separate from the workplace for long periods of time before getting thrown back into their full-time responsibilities.

Amy Beacom's approach to parental leave planning involves a conversation about whether and how an employee wishes to remain in contact with their team while on leave. Of course, those who want full separation should be able to do so. But many employees prefer to keep up to date on a project or two and don't want to fall "out of sight, out of mind." She recommends conversations where they can agree to a "keep in touch" strategy that works for them. These can range from no contact at all, a weekly phone call, a designated "work buddy" who emails every now and then, and even visits with the baby to the office.

Another important element is gradual return from parental leave. As Beth Rivera, Head of HR at Uncommon Goods explains, "Being gone and then 'boom!' 40 plus hours with the new role as a parent is very challenging. I'd recommend a softer re-entry." Jessica DeGroot of Thirdpath agrees, "You need to give a long enough parental leave and then a phased return. With return from leave- instead of going from white to black overnight, think about shifting gradually from light gray to dark gray."

For example, instead of a 6-weeks away and a hard return, you can arrange for an employee to come back two days during weeks 4 and 5, and then four days in weeks 6 and 7 before a return to full schedule. Further, now that work-from-home is more commonplace, one can also ramp up with "in person" days mixed in with "at home days." Cynthia Calvert, a Principal at Workforce 21C, recommends a more informal approach, "When people return from leave, consider core work hours when they need to be available and let other times be flexible- give them that freedom of choice."

However, you design it, a gradual re-entry allows an employee to ramp back up to full productivity while respecting the fact they are now juggling work and home more intensely than ever. A gradual approach also allows for a smooth transition in cases where you had other employees "step up" for the leave-taker's responsibilities. In most cases, this is preferable to an on-off approach.

BUILDING A CULTURE AROUND LEAVE

You can develop a world-class policy, but if your culture does not support it, it becomes a "policy in name only." This bait-and-switch is more destructive to a Whole-Person Workplace than not having the policy in the first place. Saying, "yes we offer 8 weeks parental leave," but also, "but you'd better not take it unless you want to ruin your career" is a perfect way to engender cynicism and crush engagement.

Overcoming Common Fears

The single greatest barrier for employers in offering extended parental leave, and for employees in utilizing leave, is fear. Employers fear that their workplace will be disrupted, work will fall through the cracks, and coworkers will feel unfairly burdened. Employees fear that, if they use the policy, it will derail career advancement and give them a reputation as a less-than-dedicated employee. For male employees, gender roles and social stigma add another layer of fear[20].

A friend of mine who is part of a parenting ERG at his workplace told me that their priority for this year was to de-stigmatize parental leave. While he says this is not a problem unique to his company, at some level, employees "fear that if they take two months that it would set them back." There's a perception that those who take leave are "living the good life with the baby at home, while others pick up the work."

We've already discussed many ways to create a positive culture around parental leave. Craft a good policy, communicate it widely, encourage employee use, enroll managers and coworkers in productive conversations, and frame parental leave as part of a larger suite of employee supports. Peer support and employee resource groups are important additional elements. Re-entering parents will appreciate having a group of co-workers with which they can discuss their challenges, stumbles, and triumphs. Parents of older children can help new parents better know what to expect and suggest successful strategies for maintaining career progression. Importantly, these groups are a visible manifestation that building a Whole-Person Workplace is everyone's job- not just leadership's.

Sincere Symbolic Gestures

Small symbolic gestures can also be important in communicating your care and support for new parents. Ron Friedman, in his book, *The Best Place to Work*, provides several examples of companies and their welcoming actions[21]. For example, Integrated Product Management purchases car seats for new parents, Snagajob provides a week's worth of chef-prepared meals, and Holder Construction buys teddy bears for older siblings, so they don't feel left out. Many employers provide a one-time bonus or stipend to help with baby-related expenses.

Leave-takers themselves have a responsibility for building the culture around leave. One small way to do this is through an "out-of-office" email message. For example, I emailed a friend a few months ago and received this amazing response:

Colleagues and Partners,

I am out of the office until X on Parental Leave enjoying time with the newest arrival to our family, my son X. While I am out of the office, my colleagues X and X (contact info below) will be on point to continue to lead the many projects in motion in our space. Please consider them your primary point of contact.

I am proud to work for a company that supports new parents and gives the opportunity for something as special as baby-parent bonding time. Wishing you a great start to the Summer and looking forward to reconnecting upon my return.

Messages like this demonstrate how much employees value employer support and represent an opportunity to normalize parental leave throughout one's internal and external networks.

Peer support, resource groups, and sincere symbolic actions are helpful, but building a strong culture around parental leave starts at the top through visible role modeling by leadership and upwardly-mobile employees. In short, employees need to see that those who used parental leave were able to advance in their careers and rise to positions of leadership.

Visible Leadership and Role-Modeling

In the past few years, several CEOs, including Colette Nataf of LightningAI, Mark Zuckerberg of Facebook, Katrina Lake of Stitch Fix, and Alexi Ohanian of Reddit, took extended parental leaves while making public statements about its importance. In one striking example, Olark's co-founders- CEO Ben Congleton and COO Matt Pizzimenti- both took three months' paternity leave from their small software company- at the same time! This was an intentional choice to demonstrate to their employees and their industry that fatherhood is important and that parental leave does not have to derail business success. According to Mandy Smith, Olark's director of people operations, "When employees see the CEO and COO use our parental-leave policy and have faith that it's going to work, they think, 'Hey, I can do the same thing if I need to'[22]"

It is even more impactful for employees to see mid-career professionals continue to progress after taking parental leave. For example, twelve years ago, Lynn Kraus of EY was one of their first partners to take maternity leave. Thanks to role models like her, as well as the supportive leadership she received, she can look at EY today and observe, "It is quite amazing to look at where we are now, where it's just a matter of course that we have partners who are either going on maternity or paternity leave.[23]"

More recently, Salesforce's Emily Fultz was promoted to a leadership position during her 6-month maternity leave. Before taking leave, she recalls a conversation with her supervisor in which she was told that, "'The level and quality of the work you've contributed to this team up until this point doesn't go away just because you're having a baby,' which really meant a lot.[24]" No doubt that assurance meant a lot to Fultz; it also reverberated to the rest of Salesforce's staff.

Such visible role models may be even more important for new fathers. Uhereczky and Vadkerti describe how Adidas[25] recognized this need by promoting the stories of male employees who adapted their work to their family needs through flex and parental leave and maintained their career progression. For example, they highlight the Director who worked "a 30-hour reduced schedule for seven years" and the Chief Communication Officer who "went on parental leave far longer than was the norm 20 years ago". That's the kind of leadership and role-modeling that helps you build a Whole-Person Workplace culture- one that that upholds high performance standards while valuing employees.

THE FINAL WORD

BASF's Bill Plastine, who is quoted several times in this chapter, became a new dad in 2020. His experience demonstrates how much employees value, and benefit from, well-crafted parental leave policies:

> I'm now a life-long champion of parental leave. It always baffled me how people did this without leave or just with a week of vacation. I was able to be home for two months. For three of these weeks, my leave overlapped with my wife's. It was great to have the three of us grow together, and now it helps her transition to work because she can be more confident in me.

By crafting good parental leave policy and going the extra mile to ensure leave works for everyone, you demonstrate your values, no matter if your workforce has 8 babies a day or 8 babies a decade.

THOUGHTS AND ADVICE

» Parental leave is one of the most important things you can offer in becoming a Whole-Person Workplace, as it provides support to new parents at a time they need support the most. Due to a lack of national policy, US employees depend on employers for this important benefit.

» Too many companies react to each pregnancy as a unique situation, instead of understanding that employees will have children from time to time, and they should adopt a more structured approach.

» To craft a parental leave policy that is right for your organization, you should consider employee needs, your desired culture, and potential costs and benefits.

» Be sure to include both moms and dads, birth parents and adoptive/ foster parents, as well as employees at all levels of your organization.

» You need to get the details right in terms of operational processes and inclusive communication.

» Use the time before an employee takes parental leave to plan for continuity of service and address the effects of leave on a department and coworkers.

» Think of parental leave as an opportunity for employee development- for the new parent, a colleague who may be "stepping up," and supervisors.

» Consider a gradual return policy in which the new parent ramps back up to their usual schedule through part-time schedules and/ or work-from-home.

» Ensure that parental leave is not just a "policy in name only," but that it is genuinely supported by leadership, managers, and your company culture.

» Drive culture around leave with visible role-modeling- showing that employees can take an extended leave and still advance in their careers.

CHAPTER 4 – SUPPORTING WORKING PARENTS

KAREN IS ONE OF MY star graduates from Fairleigh Dickinson University. Despite the fact that most of my HR students would accuse me of going on and on about the importance of supporting working parents, she, like most young people starting out in their careers, didn't fully internalize its importance until she started a family.

> *At first these things weren't important to me. I was young and dedicated to my career. I didn't have, need or even want balance-I was all about my job. Now that I'm a new mom, I much more clearly recognize the importance of balancing work and life. It changes your whole perspective.*

Thankfully, so far, Karen has been supported in her career and as a new mother. However, most new parents aren't so lucky.

In fact, Lauren Smith Brody, consultant and author of *The Fifth Trimester*[1], and Julia Beck, the founder and CEO of the It's Working Project[2], compellingly make the case that new parenthood, and especially new motherhood, can take a huge emotional toll.

Lauren Smith Brody reflects on her experience as a returning working mom:

> *I worked most of my career in corporate setting with other women. It was beneficial as a new parent to be working at a women's magazine. It allowed us to talk about things that weren't otherwise talked about. But this was such a competitive field. In*

general, the person who worked the hardest, longest with face-time and email time wins. It all felt very urgent. This dynamic didn't change when I became a new parent, and this was hard to reconcile with being a good mom. The energy it took to make everything seem ok was too draining.

Julia Beck reflects on this pressure returning moms feel:

When women come back, they feel they have to pretend that everything is fine, and work extra hard to make everything work without making waves. These are highly skilled women who are now a total beginner at something really important- being a working mother- something different than what they are used to being.

Projecting that everything is perfect is a sign and predictor of depression. Not being honest with yourself is extremely stressful and can be dangerous. This can damage women emotionally, and keep them out of the workplace. Postpartum depression can be debilitating and kill confidence over time. Employers need to support and even kind of enforce self-care, with access to support, post-partum experts, early childhood experts, pushing everyone towards honesty.

The previous chapter focused on parental leave- supporting employees as they become parents. While this is a particularly important time, becoming a parent is just the beginning. Once an employee comes back from parental leave, they are faced with the intense challenge of new working parenthood. With young, pre-school age children, they are likely to be juggling work and family more furiously than ever before and will face a consistently high level of parenting pressure for at least the next few years. After that, one is, of course, a parent for life and will face intense work-family challenges for at least the next eighteen years. And, despite the fact that fathers are more involved parents than ever before[3], a lot of this parenting pressure falls on mothers.

In this chapter, we will cover ways that employers can express their Whole-Person Workplace values by supporting parents with young children. We'll discuss how employers can help new parents access quality affordable child care, support breastfeeding, and combat the unconscious bias that new working mothers and visibly involved fathers face. By doing so, we build a culture where the most important life role of many employees- that of a parent- is something that is authentically valued and wholeheartedly supported.

Of course, not all employees are, want to be, or will become parents, and they deserve support in pursuing their interests and rising to their challenges, too. Providing a wide range of support for our wide range of employees is the topic of the following chapter.

SUPPORTING NEW PARENTS' CHILD CARE CONCERNS

Lauren Smith Brody states that, "the two major pain points for new parents are finance and child-care, and there's a pretty good Venn diagram of overlap between them... Because parental leave in the US is so inadequate, so many new parents are going back to work before they are physically and mentally ready."

Brody calls the very difficult transition of returning to work after having a baby "The Fifth Trimester"- three for pregnancy, the fourth during maternity leave, and the fifth being the return to work. She wrote a book on this topic and now works with employers on re-integrating returning parents in a way to validates them both as employees and as people. "If companies can carry these people through this incredibly challenging time- the benefits an organization gets in terms of engagement, retention, and economic success are very much worth the effort." Brody considers child care the most acute need of new working parents:

Childcare is a huge financial burden relative to what people earn. So much so that lower earning parents consider dropping out of the workforce, and this is most often the mom. More women stop working when they don't want to and companies don't want them to leave. If employers can think about and address the two pain points, and consider how they can offset the cost and stress involved with childcare, more new parents will stay with you.

Subsidized Child-Care

The most direct way for an employer to step up in this situation, leading with their Whole-Person Workplace values, is to subsidize child-care[4]. Many employers partner with nearby child-care facilities, negotiate discounts and guaranteed slots for employees, and subsidize employee fees. By engaging facilities close to work, you enable working parents to visit, have lunch with, or nurse their children- all while making commutes easier. Other employers provide subsidies directly to employees to use for a solution of their choice, giving them maximum flexibility to find care that works best for them.

Starbucks and Best Buy have recently expanded their child-care subsidies, demonstrating that this benefit can be extended to a wide variety of jobs and contexts[5]- not just the already privileged. Finally, while it isn't often the primary motivation, employers can accrue tax benefits for these subsidies, making this an attractive option for smaller businesses.

Only about 9% of employers offer some form of on-site child care. While this is obviously convenient for employees and has the added benefit of making it even easier for parents to visit their children, the costs and liabilities of managing these facilities can be steep[6]. On-site care may be a great option for large employers with the bulk of their employees working at a few large locations. Some noted companies like SAS, Google, Cisco, Disney Parks, and Johnson & Johnson make this work well[7]. But for most employers, a more flexible approach centered on subsidized care probably makes the most sense. As Lauren Smith Brody puts it, "An open-ended child care stipend, versus having your own center, offers a wider discretion in how they use the benefit- It's more options, more choice and more freedom." Tim Hall would call it "a less rigid form of flexibility."

In the Covid era, the need for child-care solutions is even more acute[8], as some facilities are running with reduced capacity and many schools are closed or operating in a hybrid manner. In Fall 2020, for example, my high-schooler attends in-person class Mondays, Wednesdays, and every other Friday. This is ok for us, as I'm a professor with a flexible schedule, and, well, he's 15 and can manage by himself for long stretches. But I'm comparatively lucky.

Remember my "Zoom Happy Hour" friend from Chapter 2 with two daughters under five? One has hybrid pre-kindergarten, and the other has semi-frequent part-time child care- and they had neither of these during Summer 2020. How can my friend and his wife both work outside the home? How can anyone work from home effectively in this situation? And again, my friend is also comparatively lucky- he can work from home and has resources to spend on the problem. Many employees have more severe child-care needs, cannot work remotely, and are less financially secure. Child-care subsidies and related solutions may be costly, but they are a lifeline to the whole people that we employ.

In their book[9], Uhereczky and Vadkerti describe how Adidas was creative in addressing the child-care needs of their employees. When Adidas opened a new facility in Herzogenaurach, Germany, it, in addition to hiring locally, transferred in employees from other Adidas facilities throughout the EU. Adidas knew that for these employees- many of them parents- uprooting and moving to a new city was stressful. Relocating for work often involves losing your child-care support system, including both paid child care you can trust as well as your network of friend and family support.

Recognizing this, Adidas reserved a few dozen slots at a local child care facility and at a local summer sport camp for children of their employees. This eliminated a stressor for the relocating parents, helped build community, and represented an outstanding way to show how much they care about their employees in the other important roles in their lives. Over time, Adidas opened and now operates its own in-house child-care facilities.

Back-Up Child Care

In addition to subsidized child care, many employers contract for back-up care. For example, employees at EY, who have to work but whose kids are too sick to go to school or who had their child care arrangement fall through, can arrange for an in-home child care professional to step in through EY's partnership with BrightHorizons[10]. There are several other national providers of this service, plus local options. Back-up care can give peace of mind because, as Dave Bolotsky of Uncommon Goods says, "If you can help employees avoid making these awful decisions [work or care], you then attract and retain terrific people you might otherwise lose."

Parent-Focused Shared Work Facilities

Co-working facilities designed around the needs of working mothers represents another creative approach. For example, The Wing in downtown NYC is a co-working facility where freelancers, small businesses and remote employees can work[11]. It offers the typical supports these facilities provide- conference rooms, shared use offices, phone/internet services, and printers/copiers. However, The Wing also includes an in-house café and lactation rooms. Most importantly, it is adjoined to The Little Wing, a child-care facility that offers classes, playtime drop-off, and full-time child care.

The Women's Plaza in downtown Portland takes a similar approach[12]- a full-fledged co-working facility, amenities for new mothers, attached to a child-care facility. They anticipate offering a membership model that would allow businesses to rotate employees, such as new mothers coming off maternity leave, through the space.

Times are tough right now for shared office facilities, but, one would think that post-Covid, there will be ample demand. According to Women's Plaza founder Glaucia Martin-Porath, "I would have gone back to work earlier if I had the opportunity to work and be close to my child... I would have stayed with my children if I had the opportunity to go to work and be with them and breastfeed and still be productive." These types of co-working facilities represent a creative approach to the child-care problem- perhaps your company could partner with one going forward.

Another creative solution comes from Amy Beacom of the Center for Parental Leave Leadership. She proposes that large employers with cafeterias would do well to offer take-home options. Being able to occasionally take home dinner for four- eliminating the need for grocery shopping and cooking- relieves stress and saves time. This may be especially important for working parents with young children.

Creative, Customized Child-Care Solutions

Billy Griffin of New Moon Natural Foods shares an example of what a creative Whole-Person workplace can do to support new parents- especially as a small business where you may not be able to develop a large-scale policy but can customize your approach to particular employees:

We don't necessarily have a policy for everything, but we do have a set of values, and if you build these values into your decisions, you can go above and beyond. A couple who work for us had just had a baby. Because of who they are and the type of work they did, we allowed them to bring her to work- most of the time, she was strapped on her mom's back. Yes, there are liability concerns and this approach would not be everyone's cup of tea, but this solution really suited their life. Their baby grew up here, and the family is so dedicated to us and the workplace.

In this case, this solution really worked. The beauty of it is that the couple could work the same hours together, and, as a result, could be home with their baby together- and really together. They weren't just working alternate shifts, passing the baton with a quick kiss and then bed. They could have a whole home life together. And we could help provide that for them- We didn't make them work opposite shifts, or force one of them to take a job elsewhere.

For us, the return was uber-loyalty from them. The store is built into the fabric of their lives. Five years later, they're still with us and do great work. Their child isn't here every day any more, but comes around a lot, and is like a mascot for the store. Everyone knows and loves her, and it makes the workplace feel much more like a family. Not lip service to being a family, but a real embrace of this concept.

Plus, we operate in a small town, and many of our long-term customers know our employees and also love this kid. She knows customers by name, and so many customers appreciate having seen her grow up in the store. The benefits of our choice to support our employees in what may seems like an extreme way is that we've created an authentic family environment for employees and generated commitment- and also the ripple effect among customers is profound.

This story demonstrates that if you get to know your employees and then seek creative, customized solutions for them, you can help alleviate a major stressor in their lives. By doing so, you also create a culture in which employees are recognized as whole people, generating intense employee loyalty.

SUPPORT FOR BREASTFEEDING

Many new mothers who wish to continue breastfeeding struggle with finding a functional way to express breast milk at the workplace. In fact, about four out of five American mothers start out breastfeeding[13]. However, due to several barriers- inadequate parental leave, unsupportive workplaces, poor facilities- only 60% of new mothers breastfeed (and/ or exclusively use expressed breast milk) for as long as they intended[14]. There's no shame in formula or bottle-feeding; mothers should be able to feed their children according to their preferences. A friend of mine once confided to me:

> On the whole breastfeeding thing, my employer does not have a dedicated breast feeding room. I was sharing an office with a male colleague, and honestly, I felt so uncomfortable doing it, I stopped early. Again, that's not necessarily unique to where I worked.

In fact, since 2010, the PPACA requires employers with 50 or more employees to provide "a place, other than a bathroom, that is shielded from view and free from intrusion from coworkers and the public, which may be used by an employee to express breast milk.[15]"

Some employers don't comply with this policy at all. Many employers simply convert a closet or unused office into a pumping room, doing the bare minimum to comply with the law. According to Julia Beck, "the dingy environment many employers provide- whether they do so intentionally or unintentionally- communicates how little they care about returning moms."

For example, Megan Peri[16] worked at a company with an open floor plan, whose only rooms with doors were conference rooms (almost always booked ahead of time), bathrooms, and a closet filled with server towers. She chose the closet to pump. The door didn't lock, so she taped a note on the door and used a power cord to lock the handle. "The server closet didn't actually have a wall that went all the way to the ceiling, so people could hear the machine."

Contrast this with how BirchBox, a subscription beauty product e-tailer, not only complied with this mandate, but also embraced it with authentic interest, messaging, and follow-through[17]. According to Director of Recruiting and Talent Development, Melissa Enbar, when moms return from maternity leave, they have access to peer support groups, as well as an inviting on-site lounge for pumping.

The pumping lounge has a comfortable couch and chairs, snacks, chargers for phones and laptops, and a stocked mini-fridge. The room includes a hospital-grade breast pump, so new moms don't need to lug their personal pumps to and from home (each mom has her own attachments stored in the room, in a cubby labeled with a picture of her baby). This is a fantastic way to demonstrate whole-person workplace values and show support for employees in perhaps their most important life role. The best thing is, most workplaces can replicate most of this approach. There's little excuse for forcing new mothers to pump in the server closet.

Many new mothers travel for work, so breastfeeding or pumping at the office are not options. Some employers have contracted with Milk Stork[18], a service that quickly transports breast milk in sealed, cooled containers from traveling moms back to their babies. The service can be expensive, but it is a benefit that would probably mean a lot to a targeted group of employees. Lauren Smith Brody says, "a benefit like this may not be widely used, but go a long way to acknowledge parents and add to your 'cultural bucket'."

Finally, employers can provide pre-natal, breastfeeding, and parenting classes through third parties. One such provider is the Los Angeles based Pump Station[19]. Julia Beck explains:

> During Covid, they expanded their services online. A service that was once limited geographically, is now available to anyone. Even if it's not quite as good as in-person, a 'learning to latch' class with an expert coach can be a life-saver. Why can't an employer offer these services through a third party? Doing so shows an authentic commitment to employees, and goes way beyond perfunctory box-checking.

CULTURAL SUPPORT FOR NEW PARENTS

Many I interviewed for this book recalled that, before they had kids of their own, they were often resentful of colleagues when they took leave or needed accommodations for family. It's only natural when you feel like you are putting in extra work and others are perceived as being allowed to do less.

Thankfully, there are many ways to reduce the resentment that others may feel towards accommodated working parents. Amy Beacom's and CPLL's parental leave coaching program suggests several ways to defuse resentment, perhaps even before it can take root:

» Before an impending parental leave, employees, managers, and co-workers should meet regularly to make plans for shifting workloads and responsibilities. By having clear communication ahead of time, you reduce unwanted surprises and avoid overburdening colleagues.

» It is even better if these plans can include developmental "step-up" opportunities for junior employees- that way, the parental leave is not a burden of extra work, but a valuable learning opportunity with career implications.

» Finally, Beacom recommends that returning parents show sincere gratitude to their teammates who stepped up for them- perhaps with small gifts, thank-you notes, or taking colleagues to lunch.

On a larger scale, an employer can defuse resentment by committing to being a Whole-Person Workplace for everyone. If parents are the only set of employees who get time off, flexibility, and the opportunities to leave work early, of course others will resent them (and you). From *The Fifth Trimester*:

> *Every single one of your childless peers has something in his or her personal life that she values as much as you do your baby... we all have family members, many of us have aging parents, we all have friends and we all try to have a life outside of work... If someone needs to leave early to go to the doctor, or take their child to the doctor, or their parent to the doctor [and pet to the vet], it's all the same...*

If all employees- parents or not- feel supported in their life goals and challenges, there will be less score-keeping, social comparison, and jealousy. It may sound counter-intuitive, but the best way to support new parents is to equally support your non-parent workforce. That way, the mentality changes, becoming "my employer stepped up for me when I needed it, so why shouldn't they step up for my colleague now?"

The next chapter will dive into a full range of employee supports, including educational assistance, vacation time, financial assistance, elder care, and support for volunteerism. Chapter 2's focus on maximizing workplace flexibility for as many employees as possible is also of critical importance. After all, all of our employees, no matter their specific circumstances, are whole people and need to be respected as such.

CONFRONTING IMPLICIT BIAS AGAINST CAREGIVERS

Implicit bias represents a more insidious factor than short-term resentment. There is often an unconscious prejudice against working parents- especially but not exclusively moms. Cynthia Calvert of Workforce 21C, a lawyer who often works in family responsibility discrimination law, describes this phenomenon:

> There's an implicit bias against caregivers- parents but also those dealing with elder care. That they are insufficiently committed to work, not available to take on certain tasks, not team players, and can't be part of a "work-first" culture. And for men- not masculine enough.
>
> There's a lot of assumptions- this new mother won't be able to travel, or work late nights. What if they have to be absent? These affect job assignments, which then affect career progression, compensation and training opportunities- without managers or employers always being conscious of this.
>
> For example, if a department has an opening and has to decide on a promotion. A similarly qualified mother and father both up for it. Who is this supervisor going to recommend? The woman, who he assumes will need to put family first, or the surer shot- the assumption is that the man has a wife to deal with family things.

Will he take a chance to go against the stereotype? This may not even be a conscious thought process.

We really need to battle unconsidered decision-making. Manager training in implicit bias is a good start, but we also need to examine our decision-making processes and inputs- more objective data, more people in on decision-making. And we need to examine the results of the pattern of our decisions. For example, what was the outcome of our last 10 promotion decisions?

This bias contributes to a "motherhood penalty[20]," in which mothers earn less over time than men and non-mothers.

In addition to combatting unconscious bias through training, we can also partially address this issue by reconsidering some business practices. For example, we can examine when we hold meetings and whether we hold them in-person or online. If a meeting time is too early, it can interfere with child-care drop-off. If it is too late, it can interfere with family time. Similarly, meetings can be kept shorter or include sufficient breaks to accommodate nursing or pumping moms without singling them out. More workplaces have become comfortable with Zoom meetings, or hybrid meetings with both in-person and online participants. Finally, the mix of business development activities- already transformed by Covid- can be made more inclusive. Instead of drinks on weekend evenings or golf course meetings, perhaps a broader set of activities, during more typical hours, would enable more equitable participation.

Unless you take the time to really listen and then honestly assess work processes, even the best-intentioned managers may fail to see the barriers some working mothers face. Uhereczky and Vadkerti[21] relay the story of a manager who was dismayed that his highly qualified female employee did not submit her resume for a promotion opportunity. He called to ask her why, and she stated that she was pregnant, and then cited early-morning meeting times, inflexible work, and a culture of long work hours as reasons she didn't feel she could step up. Thanks to this conversation, they brainstormed ideas for changes that would make opportunities more accessible for working mothers. These conversations take courage and may feel uncomfortable, but are necessary to confront this problem.

The motherhood penalty does not only affect women. Fathers who are visible in using leave, flex, or other family accommodations face similar pressures. In fact, multiple studies on working fathers from the Flexibility Stigma Working Group at The Center for WorkLife Law at the UC Hastings College of the Law[22], found:

» While men value work flexibility, they are reluctant to seek out flexible work arrangements because of fears of being seen as uncommitted and unmanly and of potential career consequences. These fears, unfortunately, prove to be well-founded.[23]

» Fathers who engaged in higher than average levels of childcare were subject to more workplace harassment (e.g., picked on for "not being man enough") and more general mistreatment (e.g., garden variety workplace aggression) than their low-caregiving or childless counterparts.[24]

» Men requesting family leave were perceived as uncommitted to work and less masculine; these perceptions were linked to lower performance evaluations, increased risks of being demoted or downsized, and reduced pay and rewards.[25]

» Men who interrupted their employment for family reasons earned significantly less after returning to work.[26]

WHOLE-PERSON ROLE-MODELING

Finally, creating a workplace culture around support for working parents requires leaders to act as role models. Laura Smith Brody explains how she became a role model in her sphere of influence at work.

My boss took two weeks of leave, and I wanted to be like her. 'I should be able to because she was able to.' Initially, I felt I needed to be careful about how much I talked about this. But then I decided to be super-open and transparent about my 12-week maternity leave and role as a working mother. I was lucky to be able to- because I made enough money, had a great spouse, and had a secure job as an executive.

I felt that I could make an immediate positive impact by continuing to move up and role model for others. It helped others see what was possible, and I think helped retain people, made people glad to come to work, by being up front and approachable on these topics. It took up some time, but I really wanted to show that this is good for business and was good for me, in my career and things I did later on.

THE FINAL WORD

In the end, we want to address the concerns of all our employees. For too long, the concerns of new parents, and especially new mothers, were shunted to the side. The needs of new parents need to be taken out of hiding in the dingy server closet and made a priority. By doing so, we can go a long way to creating a Whole-Person Workplace, perhaps even one in which a new mom can work with her baby strapped on her back

THOUGHTS AND ADVICE

» Parents of babies and young children face intense work-family juggles. Whole-Person Workplaces need to support these employees at this challenging time in their lives.

» Many women returning to work post-baby feel enormous pressure to hide their struggles.

» Finding and affording quality child care is a major stressor for new parents. Many employers subsidize child care, often at nearby child-care facilities, as a way to support parents.

» On-site child care is more expensive and less common but can maximize convenience for employees and allow them to spend time during the day with their kids.

» During Covid times, many families struggle with inconsistent access to child-care and rotating school schedules, making the need for viable child-care solutions even more acute.

» You can also consider creative solutions, such as reserving child-care and summer camp slots for employees, partnering with local co-working facilities, and arranging for back-up care solutions.

» Many new mothers end up discontinuing breastfeeding before they intended. This is often due to workplace barriers, such as short parental leaves and a lack of adequate facilities for pumping.

» Designing a comfortable, attractive space for pumping is a relatively easy and straightforward way to signal support for new mothers. Other supports, such as milk delivery and post-natal classes, are also helpful.

» Non-parents may resent accommodations for working parents-if their needs and concerns are not addressed and respected on an equal footing. Proper planning for post-parental leave return should help this situation by clarifying responsibilities, identifying developmental opportunities, and building in ways for new parents to thank their colleagues for stepping up for them.

» Implicit bias against mothers and caregivers can result in a "motherhood penalty" that restricts career and earning opportunities. These often-unconscious prejudices can be addressed through manager training, as well as examining decision-making criteria and outcomes.

» Fathers who make use of flex, leave, and other family accommodations face similar pressures.

» Visible role-modeling by leaders who have been able to make work and parenthood work is essential for building culture around support for working parents.

» While the needs of working parents should be addressed, it is important that parental support represents just one facet of a whole-person workplace approach that addresses the priorities and challenges of all employees.

CHAPTER 5 – A WIDE RANGE OF SUPPORTS FOR A WIDE RANGE OF EMPLOYEE CONCERNS

THE PRIOR TWO CHAPTERS focused on addressing the needs of working parents. But, of course, not all employees are, want to be, or will become parents, and they deserve support in pursuing their interests and rising to their challenges, too.

A 2018 survey by Deloitte[1] demonstrated that all employees, but especially Millennials and Gen Z, want to bring their whole selves to work and do not want to leave their lives outside the office or factory doors. Yes, they are employees, but, importantly, they are also parents, bakers, volunteers for environmental causes, friends, "weekend warrior" athletes, and dog-parents. Increasingly, these younger generations have asserted their needs and won't stay long at companies who do not support them as whole people.

Elizabeth Hall of Cambia Health perhaps says it best, "You need to offer a range of support so everyone can feel they belong in the workplace." After all, every employee is a whole person, and their priorities and challenges need to be respected and addressed.

In this chapter, we will discuss various types of benefits and programs that can help us address the variety of challenges that our workforce faces. While thorough, this chapter is by no means comprehensive- the possibilities of how you support employees are literally endless because every employee is unique.

This chapter will focus on five specific categories of support: time for life, support for those caring for older family members, support for volunteerism, educational assistance, and financial assistance programs. Employee health and wellness programs get their own chapter later on. Before diving into these issues, the first step is to better understand what your employees need.

UNDERSTANDING EMPLOYEE NEEDS

Delta Emerson of canyouhearus consulting puts it plainly, "We have to do as good a job listening to our employees as we do with our clients and prospects." Every Whole-Person Workplace needs to implement a thoughtful process for gauging employee needs and concerns. Julia Beck of the It's Working Project goes even further:

> It starts with listening. You need to hear from everyone in your community. Stories are important, and if you can ask members of your workforce to share their experiences- through pregnancy, as a new parent, elder care, other issues- this has an impact. Then have them become part of task force to gather information and propose changes. This way, you get more of the truth and show your people you care and are listening. Active listening, in itself, is a form of commitment. Policies that haven't gone through the people who have the need or experience with that need can be counterproductive. You need to show authentic interest to craft policy.

There are lots of ways to listen to employees and turn that attention into action. For smaller companies, it is comparatively easy to check the pulse of your workplace and understand individual employee needs. Chris Geschickter, CHRO of Johnstone Supply states:

> Here, I know all 140 employees. I know who they are, what they do, their families, their needs. I can relate to each of them on a personal level. For a smaller company like ours, maybe we can't

create all the big formal policies like a large employer can, but we can really understand and address each employee's needs, assess how things are going, and adjust quickly.

Billy Griffin, founder and president at New Moon Natural Foods, with 90 employees, agrees:

The big difference for a small business is that you always have the advantage of being nimble. You can pivot more quickly than the big boys. You won't be burdened with a large, cookie-cutter policy. You can better recognize that every employee is different, and can customize to specific employee situations and experiences. Then you serve them, you retain them and they love you for it. Employees feel truly seen and you can address the emotional side of the employer-employee relationship.

Larger companies can't always have such direct conversations with all their employees. However, they can gain valuable information through employee surveys[2], focus groups[3], and exit interviews[4]. These are important but need to be supplemented with personal contact with a wide cross-section of employees. As an HR executive at a national pharmacy chain told me, "You have to really listen. Surveys are great, but not enough. Leaders and HR need to engage widely, and managers need to listen and then speak up for their teams. By doing so, this become part of your strategy and culture- and it's not just top-down planning."

In their book[5], Uhereczky and Vadkerti recommend creating a profile of your workforce to give you an idea of which support programs may be most relevant. For example, they suggest looking at the number and percentages of employees that fit these following categories: Close to retirement; New parents; Parents of multiple children; Parents of children with special needs; Responsible for elderly parents; Experiencing health challenges; Do not have nearby family; Are active in their community. In addition, you should be tracking things like engagement, stress, retention, and use of available benefits, so you can craft policies to address these concerns.

Of course everyone deserves to be treated like an individual, but workforce profiles can give you an idea of the types of programs you might want to emphasize. For example, if your workforce consists mainly of 20-somethings right out of college, you may want to provide benefits that help them with student loans, foster development opportunities, and respect time for a social life. If you have a workforce with lots of parents with young children, you can emphasize leave, flexibility, and childcare support. If you have a largely middle-aged workforce, perhaps support for finances and elder care come to the forefront.

In fact, Intuit- the software company behind QuickBooks and TurboTax- presents its menu of employee benefits arranged by employee age and life stage[6]. While they emphasize health and financial planning throughout, employees at different life stages are given advice about targeted policies, such as child-care, retirement planning, and wellness.

Once you assess the range of your employees' challenges, it is important to follow through and make sure your employees know you take their concerns seriously and are turning them into action. Chris Geschickter of Johnstone Supply provides important insight:

> You have to ask- Are you really addressing their needs or just what you think their needs are? We recently conducted our annual employee engagement survey. We took our results at group level and region by region. We met as an executive team to talk through the results. We came up with three changes, shared these plans with employees to let know what we are doing in response to their feedback, and are committed to maintaining transparency and accountability.

Dave Bolotsky, CEO of Uncommon Goods, adds that once you talk to employees, it's okay to test out solutions. "Maybe test out something like a new way to schedule or something to see how it works out before a full-company roll-out." Pilot-testing is a great way to ensure that you are offering what employees need and to make adjustments before wide implementation.

SUPPORTING TIME FOR LIFE

Perhaps the most direct way we can support employees is to allow them the time they need to attend to their life challenges. By providing paid time off (PTO) and encouraging its use, you give employees the space they need to craft custom-fit, "less rigid" ad-hoc solutions to their issues. Time is so valuable that 80% of surveyed job seekers said they would prefer job opportunities with generous or unlimited PTO over higher-paid opportunities[7] (flexible and remote work were also rated at a similar level).

Supporting Time for Life Through Vacation Policy

Despite this preference, many employees don't get or use sufficient PTO. There is an epidemic of unused vacation in US. In fact, in 2018, American workers failed to use almost 768 million vacation days, eschewing about 27% of the days they earned[8]. On its face, this seems absurd. However, there are several reasons that explain this phenomenon.

Many employees feel pressure to be "all in" at their workplace and to keep up with internal competition, so they do not use their time off. Others feel indispensable, or may have been put into situations in which they are the sole employee responsible for an important client or a critical work process (Chapter 6 discusses how to redesign work flow to minimize this pressure).

And, while Roger Dow, the President and CEO of the U.S. Travel Association, has a vested interest in getting people to take their vacation time and travel the country, he makes an important point, "When I see how many vacation days went unused, I don't just see a number- I see 768 million missed opportunities to recharge, experience something new and connect with family and friends."

So, our challenge as employers who want to support employee's time for life is twofold. First, offer an appropriate (or even generous) amount of paid time off, and then encourage (or at least stop discouraging) its use.

An Example of a Whole-Person Vacation Policy

One model company for PTO is the global accounting and finance firm EY[9]. While EY employees work hard and many frequently travel for work, they earn generous PTO. Based on position and tenure, EY employees receive somewhere between 3 and 6 weeks PTO. Additionally, they get 12 paid holidays, including 4-day weekends for Memorial Day, Labor Day and Thanksgiving. Finally, EY closes its offices completely for the week of July 4th and the last week of December through January 1[10]. This PTO is in addition to generous paid parental and family care leave.

I'd like to highlight a few features of how EY designed its policy for maximum effectiveness and uptake.

First, they offer more days off than most employers (but perhaps not as much as Netflix which provides "unlimited" PTO). An employee with 4 weeks paid vacation can use it in many different ways. They can take two long vacations; they can take multiple shorter ones. One model I like comes from a friend of mine who works at EY.

Many people I know use their vacation days only for full blown family vacations. I realized that I was leaving days on the table, so I decided to make a change. Every winter, I take at least 3-4 individual days off to go skiing with my buddies. It's a just a day trip, I don't miss time with the family (kids are in school, wife is at work), and it refreshes me for the rest of the week. I do similar days in the summer for golf. This really works well for me.

In addition, by turning 3-day weekends into 4-day weekends, EY employees can get the jump on others in going on vacation. Where I live, being able to leave for a holiday weekend on the Jersey Shore on

Thursday night or Friday morning as opposed to Friday evening saves you hours of soul-crushing Garden State Parkway traffic. Many who would not normally choose to travel on busy holiday weekends now feel able to, given the extra time. And if one is not traveling, a day off during a typical work day opens up opportunities for errands, doctor's visits, and home repairs that would otherwise have to be squeezed in during more crowded times.

EY recently implemented a "use it or lose it" policy for their PTO, meaning that vacation time needs to be used by a certain end-date or else it is forfeited[11]. This proved controversial, as there are two sides to this issue. On the one hand, we want to encourage use of PTO. On the other, we don't want to be punitive, especially as some employees may want to "save up" vacation days for things like honeymoons or to care for family members. However, "use it or lose it" does have one clear advantage- more people use their vacation time.

Supporting Time for Life Through Full-Company Breaks

Further, I really like the idea of a full company shut-down (of course, this may not be possible for many workplaces). Some of the main reasons people do not take available leave are that they fear falling behind or dread the work that piles up for them for when they return. Worse, if you are on vacation when all your coworkers are not, you'll sometimes get barraged by emails, texts, and phone calls. By contrast, if the whole office is away, there is less pressure to stay "always on" during what should be down time.

Ginny Kissling, Global President and COO of Ryan, described the relief she felt during a full-company break:

> When we are recognized by Fortune as a Best Company to Work For, we thank team members by taking a full-company summer break. This was so impactful to me and unlike anything I experienced before. I'd had two maternity leaves in my life, but

never felt that same relief. I actually got to take a week off of the weight of piled-up emails and pressure to keep things moving. Because pretty much everyone had that time off, there were very few emails, and any that came in were greeted with a celebratory 'Fortune 100 out-of-office message.'

Honestly, it was hard for us in the upper levels to mentally turn things off, but leadership on this issue is so important. I helped the CEO on messaging- making sure that everyone was on the same page, and that no one, even leadership, should be processing emails. We needed to respect the week off for all of us. And only the most urgent client issues could get through. To me, I thought- is this too good to be true? As a leader, I had to have the self-control to set the example.

Kissling makes another important point that leadership needs to signal its support for true unconnected time off, not just in word, but in action. Professor Alyssa Westring recalls a conversation with a senior leader who realized she was not serving as that example:

She would always tell her employees to unplug after hours and to take all their vacation time. But they saw her working all the time, emailing 24/7, and assumed they had to as well. Many didn't want to get promoted because they saw her hours! When she finally realized she had unconsciously shifted the culture it was profound realization for her. The choices leaders make affect others in terms of time use and of prioritizing life.

I should note that 2021 may be an odd year in terms of PTO. Many employees did not use vacation time in 2020- after all, it was very difficult to travel, especially during summer months. As a result, many employees will have additional accumulated days for 2021 and beyond. Also, Covid-era work-from-home, with all its resultant work-family challenges, is extremely stressful. However, many workers are reluctant to take time off because: (a) they'd still be home anyway, and (b) they understand their continued employment could be precarious during these hard economic times.

Lots of these employees are prime candidates for burnout and should be encouraged to take at least occasional time off. Robert Russo of Bristol-Myers Squibb told me that BMS implemented a handful of company-wide days off during 2020 in order to combat burnout. What a great idea.

In short, Whole-Person Workplaces should offer significant PTO, design their policies to encourage use, and make sure that leadership is sending the intended signals. Time off is so important for relaxation, recharging, and allowing our employees their most important need- time for life outside of work.

Supporting Time for Life Through Paid Sick Leave

One of the most important things we can do for employee health and wellness is provide sufficient paid time off for sick leave- both for sick employees and for them to care for sick family members. As the owner of a small custom furniture manufacturer told me:

> I don't want someone coming into work sick. First, it's not right for them. I also don't want them getting others sick. I also don't want them coming in worried about their sick kids. In this business, a lack of focus can lead to a mistake, and that means really expensive re-work. Also, it can cause an accident and hurt workplace safety. A few days of paid sick leave reduces all these risks.

For Billy Griffin of New Moon Natural Foods, the Covid pandemic reinforced the importance of paid sick leave:

> It's a tricky balance for hourly employees who don't earn a lot to stay home if they're sick. Of course, we want them to stay home, but it's harder for them if they aren't getting paid. Missing three

days of pay is 30% of their expected paycheck. That's a big deal to a lot of people.

Through Covid, we had to be more accommodating, and we realized that we can survive these things and absorb that cost. This led us to increasing PTO and paid sick time for all employees. We can give a buffer and take care of people in different ways. I wasn't sure we could so I never really explored it. It turns out we can.

Currently, there is no federal mandate for paid sick leave, meaning that employers are largely responsible for setting their own policies. Many states and municipalities have enacted laws requiring employers to allow employees to accrue up to 5 paid sick days a year[12]. For Whole-Person Workplaces, this should be a no-brainer- even a small investment in PTO helps create a healthier workplace, benefitting both workers and employers.

ELDER CARE AND THE PANINI GENERATION

There has been a lot of media attention paid to the "sandwich generation" who face the dual pressure of raising children while caring for aging parents[13]. Ginny Kissling of Ryan sums up the pressures this generation faces, "Caring for children, an aging parent, an illness in your family, all these things cause stress that keeps you from being focused at work or at home. You're not at peak because of the stress associated with caring."

Julia Beck of the It's Working Project thinks the sandwich metaphor does not go far enough (and she's right):

It's more like the panini generation. A sandwich, but also hotter, more squeezed, under more pressure. There's a whole generation of people scraping the melted cheese from our sides!

Cynthia Calvert of Workforce 21C adds:

There's not as much understanding by employers on elder care, as opposed to childcare. With child care, you know there's an end point when you get your employee back. And there's the whole perpetuating the species thing. Elder care can go on for decades. It's also more difficult to talk about- 'how's your dad's diabetes?' without crossing a legal line. By and large, employers aren't as sympathetic.

Of course, work flexibility would enable many paninis to find the time to attend to their dual responsibilities. Other employers set aside paid time off to care for family members or roll family care into their overall PTO banks. For example, EY extends 10 paid days to care for family members[14]. Beyond that, you can support your employees as they scrape off the cheese by providing peer support groups and support services or by partnering with care facilities and subsidizing elder care[15]. Back-up elder care is also a useful option[16]. For example, Ginny Kissling describes one benefit Ryan offers:

We contract with an EAP and, this is my favorite- there's a hotline employees can call that helps them review their medical bills, and help with troubles with Medicare payments. They helped me and my dad review his bills to make sure everything was in order- they can get so complicated with insurance and Medicare and all. This was financial help, sure, but it really was a way to eliminate stress and get me peace of mind that everything was in order and my dad was taken care of.

Simply listening to employees can present creative and custom-fit solutions. For instance, an HR executive at a national pharmacy chain told me of her personal experience:

My mother who lived in a different country was not doing well, and I had to go to be with her. My employer was totally

*understanding and helped me arrange everything I needed to be
there, while working remotely, for about two months. I mean, who
else would do that? Why would I ever look for a job anywhere else?*

That's the kind of commitment you generate when you demonstrate
genuine care for employees as whole people.

SUPPORTING EMPLOYEES' DESIRE TO VOLUNTEER

Most people have causes they care about and support. But with the time
demands of work and life, many of us regret that we don't have as much
bandwidth as we'd like to support these causes. By supporting employees'
desires to volunteer, contribute, and give back to their communities, you
are sending an important signal- that you care about their priorities, even
if these interests have little to do with work.

Tapping into employee values can be a powerful motivator and can
lend emotional heft to the employer-employee bond. Further, support
for volunteerism and for employees' philanthropic efforts helps increase
morale, create a positive work atmosphere, and can even improve your
employer brand[17]. The Society for Human Resource Management
estimates that about 26% of employers have programs to support charity
and volunteerism[18].

Supporting your community doesn't need to be a formal policy. Take
the example of Jugtown Country Store, from co-owner Tom Prendergast:

*During the pandemic, one of our employees came to us with
an idea to put out a tip jar, but that all the tips would go to
the local food bank. We all thought that was a great idea, and
was incredibly generous- our employees could have benefitted
from the tips themselves, but they thought it was more important
to help others in our community. We decided we'd support this
employee initiative. Now, every Sunday, a portion of our profits
are donated to that food bank. So far, we've raised and donated
enough to provide 20,000 meals. It just shows the heart that*

people have, and the good you can do when you give them the opportunity to act on it at work.

Donating Time and Money

One direct way to support your employees' desire to contribute to others is through a donation matching program[19]. When an employee makes a donation to a legitimate 5013b charity (some employees place restrictions on the types of charities they support to avoid religious or political complications), the employer matches that contribution, in whole or in part, or perhaps up to a maximum amount. In fact, employers as diverse as PepsiCo, Johnson & Johnson, and Exxon-Mobil provide 2:1 or even 3:1 matches. By providing a match, you show employees that their priorities are your priorities, too, and that you are willing to provide tangible financial support to something that is important to them.

As employees are often too busy to volunteer their time to community or charitable organizations, you can also support them by donating time. Many companies provide paid time off, often ranging from a day to a week, for employees to engage in charitable activities[20]. As with donation matching, you are tangibly supporting their priorities. By giving the gift of time, you are also enabling workers to feel the satisfaction that comes from altruistic work. For both them and you, working for a cause is more personally meaningful than just making a financial donation. Uncommon Goods, a New York based online retailer, provides paid days off for volunteerism and recently rolled out corporate charity match. According to CHRO Beth Rivera, "Volunteerism during a work day and doing some good really helps build our community."

Developing Employees and Workplace Culture Through Volunteerism

Further, many companies see volunteerism as a developmental opportunity for employees- for example, a junior employee who helps run a local fund-raising campaign may develop planning, communication, and leadership skills. These skills can then be brought to bear in the workplace and contribute to motivation and to advancement opportunities[21].

Finally, many employers engage in company-wide charity or community events. These events can help build team cohesiveness while emphasizing company values. They can be powerful bonding opportunities. Ginny Kissling, Global President and COO at Ryan LLC, describes their annual company-wide charity event:

> *On our company anniversary in mid-July, we hold an all-employee volunteer event to benefit the North Texas Food Bank. We used to be able to do this all together as a company, but now that we've grown so large, we have to split our volunteer days into shifts of 100 employees. It's a great feeling to give back to our community, and community service is a big part of our company culture. It is also really satisfying to see the results of our efforts in giving back.*

Conagra Foods does not hold a single event; instead, they support volunteer opportunities year-round. Lisa Evans, Director of Talent Development, describes their program:

> *We have an Employee Resource Group that helps plan lots of opportunities for volunteerism and fund-raising. We also get our employees' families involved. One time, we raised funds to donate new computers to local schools, and then we went to those schools to volunteer- including installing and setting up those workstations. One time, my kids and I were able to bond together when we painted rooms at a school. It's a great way to involve families in a values-based way.*

Employer-sponsored events provide opportunities for employees to act in accordance with their values- an amazing gift we can give them. These events also relieve individual employees from having to arrange for their own volunteer opportunities, freeing up more time and mental bandwidth. For example, one busy working father told me:

> *One of the best ways to continue to give back to your community is to find a way to do it with or through your employer. As a family man, I appreciate the importance of maximizing my time. My firm is committed to corporate responsibility, and I've been encouraged to give back - even during work hours.*

Finally, many job-seekers state a strong preference for employers that reflect their values. Supporting volunteerism is a great way to stand out in the marketplace. In fact, this is so important that The Fortune 100 contains a sub-list for the 50 Best Workplaces for Giving Back[22] and Glassdoor highlights employers that support volunteerism[23].

Employer branding and recruitment advantages aren't usually the primary motivations behind support for volunteerism, but a little well-earned PR never hurt anyone. This is yet another demonstration that Whole-Person Workplace values, including support for employees' desire to give back to causes that are important to them, benefit everyone.

SUPPORT FOR EMPLOYEE LEARNING AND DEVELOPMENT

The work world is very different than it was a generation ago. Because of rapid globalization, technological innovations, and the head-spinning rate of change, it is increasingly rare for an employee to work in a single career path for a single employer than ever before.

Now, in order to succeed at almost any long-term job or career, one needs to become adept at lifelong learning- ongoing, voluntary, and self-motivated pursuit of knowledge for personal or professional reasons[24]. While employees are largely responsible for managing their own protean careers and ensuring their skills match employer needs, there are many things Whole-Person Workplaces can and should do to support lifelong learning. By doing so, we tap into employee motivation to develop new skills.

Supporting lifelong learning is also good business- when we upskill our workforce, we'll get better performance. Further, employees who are satisfied with their development and career progression are far more likely to stay with you, rather than seek employment elsewhere[25].

Supporting Learning Through Formal Education and Educational Benefits

Employers can directly invest in employee education by paying for or subsidizing tuition for college or targeted master's programs. For example, my business school frequently partners with area businesses to teach specialized master's programs for a cohort of their employees, often at their offices. Companies can also set up Education Assistance Programs to make direct payments to educational institutions or, more commonly, to reimburse employee costs[26]. These programs can get complex, so please seek specialist advice before moving forward.

Bill Plastine of BASF discusses the educational benefits they offer:

Our manufacturing employees make great use of our tuition reimbursement programs- which can be used for colleges, technical schools, online courses, certificate programs, and community colleges- night programs in the skilled trades. Because we have lots of different types of employees, we try to extend a wide range across the whole organization and then people can choose what works for them. At one facility, we have a partnership with a local community college- they can go there for free and take courses in specialized areas that are relevant to the work at our site. For us, skill-building is very important.

Further, two recent employer programs made headlines. First, in 2014 Starbucks announced a partnership with Arizona State University, paying the tuition for employees to pursue online bachelor's degrees[27]. This benefit extends to part-time employees, and Starbucks only requires a few months' tenure before becoming eligible. In the 5 years since the program began, about 12,000 Starbucks employees have enrolled.

For Starbucks, with a largely young workforce, being able to extend this benefit helps them with recruitment, engagement and retention[28]. Maybe a Starbucks ASU graduate moves on after they earn their degree, but, in an industry with a 200%-300% employee turnover rate, keeping a barista for 4 or 5 years gives them a huge advantage. Some graduates move up into management, and I bet all become loyal customers for life.

Similarly, Amazon offers a program in which it reimburses up to 95% of tuition, fees and textbook costs for its hourly workers to pursue certificate programs and associates degrees[29]. In fact, Amazon explicitly states they want to help these employees embark on higher-paying careers, even if this means moving on from Amazon. Again, in an industry marked by high turnover, this benefit more than returns their initial investment and represents Whole-Person Workplace values. While it is likely you don't share Starbucks' or Amazon's education budgets, their examples show that direct educational assistance can be a valued benefit for all types of employees.

Supporting Learning Through Certificate Programs

You can also consider more targeted certificate programs. These can be very useful in ensuring employees are up to date in their field and ready to move up. Certificate programs require less employee time and fewer budgetary dollars while still providing impact. For example, a company with a moderately-sized HR department may be wise to pay for these employees to attend an 8-week online prep course for the Society for Human Resource Management's PHR Certification exam, as well as their materials and testing fees.

By doing so, they'd upskill their department, enable employees to earn a valuable credential, and demonstrate their genuine interest in employee development. Almost every specialized career path is associated with a professional organization and relevant certificate programs. You may want to consider which mix is right for you.

Over the past few years, a wider variety of targeted certification programs have been developed. One promising example comes from LinkedIn Learning[30]. This is a suite of short, usually inexpensive (some cost as little as $30) online learning programs, in a wide array of fields and applications. When someone completes a program, they can attach that certification badge to their profile and resume. Employers can purchase a business account for their employees to access these materials. Programs like this enable you to offer a flexible, cost-effective program in which employees select their own learning topics, providing a just-in-time approach to supporting lifelong learning.

Of course, many larger companies have robust employee development departments that offer programs and closely manage career tracks. These are obviously very important, but direct investments in formal education or online professional development are smart ways to supplement these activities. Employers can further supplement their in-house department by offering informal learning opportunities, such as mentoring programs, on-the-job shadowing, and informal "lunch and learn" programs.

Supporting Development by Supporting Employee Initiatives

As we've already discussed, one of the major benefits of being a Whole-Person Workplace is that we enable our employees to bring their whole selves to work, and that includes bringing their creativity and new ideas.

Allagash Brewery in Portland, Maine, provides an instructive example. Allagash sets aside brewing vats for employees to experiment with their own recipes through their Pilot Beer Program[31]. Employees develop and brew small amounts for their coworkers to sample. Based on peer feedback, some recipes are produced in larger batches for local brew pubs, and depending on customer reaction, some go into full distribution. In fact, their fourth best-selling product, their Saison, was developed through this program.

I love this program because most people don't work for a craft brewery just for the money. For most Allagash employees, craft beer is also a passion. Enabling employees to explore and express this passion recognizes and validates them as whole people, including their minds and hearts and taste buds. The Pilot Beer Program also supports employee development and learning, as it helps participating employees better understand the intricacies of the brewing process, marketing, and distribution.

Recognizing employee creativity doesn't necessarily require a formal process. At Jugtown Country Store, for example, employees have come up with ideas for reducing waste, recognizing co-workers, and, as discussed earlier in this chapter, supporting their community.

Most employees want to grow, learn, and expand their opportunities. Whole-Person employers can support their employees by offering them avenues to reach these goals. By doing so, you also signal your genuine commitment to their development.

ADDRESSING WHOLE-PERSON CONCERNS THROUGH FINANCIAL ASSISTANCE

Of course the most important financial benefit an employer can provide is a good, livable wage (see Chapter 7). Beyond this, many employers have crafted creative solutions to helping employees with their finances, particularly for long-term capital appreciation and for help with the more stressful aspects of employees' financial lives.

Financial Assistance Through Retirement and Long-Term Investment

One could write an entire book on capital appreciation programs, such as 401k[32] plans- and this is not that book. The fiduciary and disclosure regulations involved with 401k plans are complex and vary with tax law[33]. You should consult with compensation and legal experts when setting up or re-evaluating your program. I want to highlight just a few elements of this benefit that communicate Whole-Person Workplace values.

Traditional capital appreciation programs often involve partnering with an investment firm and facilitating pre-tax contributions from employees into their choice of offered investment funds. Even if this is all you do, you are helping employees by providing them a way to make tax-deferred contributions, making long-term investment easier. Most of the investment firms you could partner with also provide free or heavily discounted financial counseling services.

A common way to enhance 401k plans is to match employee contributions, at least up to a point. For example, an employer might match the first 3% of employee salary contributed to retirement plans. The employee puts 3% of their income, tax deferred into their investment fund, and then you, as the employer, contribute an amount equal to 3% of their salary into their investment. It is literally free money for employees, very helpful and very appreciated.

Matching makes sense from an employer point of view as well, as your contributions reduce your payroll taxes, while encouraging employees to invest, reducing your payroll taxes further[34]. In some industries, you can stand out as an employer by offering a match; in others, employers who don't provide matches are at a comparative disadvantage in recruitment.

That said, matching contributions cost a significant amount of money. A 3% match, for example, increases your overall payroll by, well not quite 3% (because of the tax advantages). Obviously, helping employees invest for retirement and, better yet, making your own matching contribution towards that goal are important ways to show how much you value employees- even if they reap most of the benefits after they are no longer working for you.

It was long assumed that good retirement plans and other financial benefits, such as life insurance and quality health insurance, were only provided to already privileged white-collar employees. However, retailers, such as Costco[35] and Trader Joes, extend these benefits to hourly employees and to both full-time and part-time workers- and even include a 401k match. One can make the case that retirement plans are particularly important for lower-paid employees who have traditionally had less access to vehicles for long-term wealth accumulation and for passing wealth to the next generation.

Financial Assistance Through Student Loan Assistance

I work at a private university, and I can tell you that one of the major concerns of today's college graduates is student debt. In pre-Covid 2020, it was estimated that about 44.7 million Americans owed a collective $1.56 trillion in student loans- an average debt of just under $33,000[36]. For many recent grads, this debt weighs on them like an anvil. They feel like they cannot start building wealth, move out of their parent's homes, or even think about starting a family. Some opt for high-paying jobs over opportunities or employers that might be better long-term fits.

Imagine how freeing it would feel for these young college graduates if their employer helped them with their student loans. I suspect it would feel like being lifted out of a pressurized panini press. While only about 4% of employers offer student loan assistance to its employees[37], it is becoming more common[38], and the need for these programs, I think, will only increase.

Student loan assistance can take several forms. In some cases, the employer buys and consolidates loans, and then passes on a lower interest rate to employees. In others cases, an employer adds a match (similar to a 401k match) to the employee's student loan repayments. Some simply apply a forced savings option[39] and redirect student loan payments directly from employee paychecks, helping employees maintain the financial discipline to repay loans in a timely manner.

Employer subsidies are considered taxable income, somewhat limiting the impact for employees. However, if a program provides a match or a reduced interest rate, this financial benefit becomes even more impactful. Student loan assistance is most appropriate for firms that largely recruit and hire employees straight from college and face stiff competition in doing so. It is little surprise that a "Big 4" accounting/financial firm like PriceWaterhouseCoopers[40], for example, extends this benefit.

Financial Assistance for Major Life Events

One particularly generous approach to financial assistance comes from online retailer Boxed and the Whole-Person Workplace values of its CEO, Chieh Huang (you may remember their unlimited parental leave policy discussed in Chapter 3). His priority is helping employees pay for life-altering events.

Boxed pays the college tuition for all employees' children[41]. One grateful employee, the father of a high-school senior said, "When I realized the policy applied to me, I breathed a huge sigh of relief. When I told my son, he said, 'I didn't think people did things like that'." (On a related note, many employers assist employees with college savings accounts, often known as 529 plans[42].)

Boxed also reimburses employees for wedding expenses up to $20,000[43]. Huang started this perk when an hourly employee was running himself ragged with a second job to both care for his ill mother and save for his wedding- but was still falling behind. One day, the normally stoic employee broke down crying and left work early. After talking to him about his situation, Huang decided to take that pressure off him by paying for the wedding- leading to a new benefit for all employees.

Clearly, Boxed puts its money behind its priorities- unlimited parental leave, college tuition and wedding costs are not cheap. Huang says that paying for such life-altering events represents a truer way to support employees than the more publicized perks you hear a lot about in the business press: "Every company has to decide what they want to focus on, and for us it's paying for these life-altering events for our employees... It's not the cheapest program, but... there are no beer kegs, ping-pong tables or free lunches... we use our money to fund what we think are really impactful and meaningful." He also notes that fewer than 10 full-time employees have voluntarily left the company since it was founded in 2013.

Relatedly, employers can provide special tax-free grants to employees during times of crisis or natural disasters or- if an employee faces severe economic hardship- through crisis financial assistance funds[44]. The need for these funds have obviously become more acute during the Covid pandemic[45]. In short, an employer can set up its own fund or partner with an outside not-for-profit, and then extend grants to employees with hardships. These funds can be tricky to set up and run but provide great help to employees in need- representing a strong manifestation of Whole-Person values.

Perhaps you are not in the financial position to do what Boxed does, but there are probably many ways you can help your employees with major financial concerns. Billy Griffin at New Moon Natural Foods demonstrates how a smaller employer can step up for employees when needed:

> We had one employee with a chronic health condition who occasionally landed in the hospital. Our employment contract, of course, is just at-will employment, but we stepped up for her. She is a strong employee and a manager, so we continued to pay her during her extended time off. We looked at this as an investment, not a cost. I visited her in the hospital and delivered the news personally. Not only did she appreciate the financial relief, but the gesture itself sold her on how awesome her workplace is. For years now, she has continued to be one of our best and, not coincidentally, most loyal employees.
>
> Similarly, at one point, my wife and I were going to sell or trade in an old car of ours, probably getting around $1200 for it. But we had an employee who needed a car and was having trouble saving up for one. We gave it to her. She was elated- and is still driving it. The way we see it, the car cost us an extra 75 cents an hour for one year for that employee- it really wasn't too much of a burden to help take care of a valued employee and do the right thing for her when she needed help. That car meant vastly more to her than the money ever would to us. And now, she's a

manager and always talks to employees and customers about how well we took care of her. Further, by having a caring attitude modeled toward her, she's become a more caring manager to her staff and helps spread positive word of mouth about the store. At $1200, who wouldn't buy that for their business?

Of course, one important solution, which we will discuss in detail in Chapter 7, is to pay your employees a more livable wage. Beyond that, think about the major financial stressors that you, your friends, your family, and your employees face. Now think about how much relief you and they would feel to have that pressure taken away. What an impactful way to help your employees with a major life challenge, while engendering the kind of gratitude and reciprocity that will help your business thrive.

THE FINAL WORD

Employees face a host of pressures and challenges in their lives. Some may feel like they are being squeezed from all sides- like a sandwich being pressed down in a panini maker, oozing melted cheese all over. Every employee's set of life challenges are unique. By truly listening to employees and then creating solutions that provide them more time for life, help in caring for aging parents, support for volunteering, educational assistance, and financial help for important life events, we are well on our way to creating a Whole-Person Workplace that addresses the full range of employee concerns.

IDEAS AND ADVICE

» While it is important to support working parents, all of our employees have life challenges and priorities worthy of our consideration.

» It is imperative to listen to employee concerns, so that you can craft policies, programs, and informal accommodations that are maximally targeted, useful, and appreciated.

» Employee surveys, focus groups, exit interviews, and workforce profiles can be effective ways to collect information about employee concerns. Supervisors, leaders, and the HR department also need to consistently interact with employees to better understand their situations.

» Getting employees involved in planning and rolling out solutions is a good way to ensure your policies match real employee concerns.

» Supporting employees' need for time outside of work is crucial, as it allows employees to create their own solutions for their circumstances, and to find time to relax and recharge.

» Even when companies offer generous PTO policies, many employees fail to make use of their available leave- usually owing to fears of career or reputational consequences. Employers need to craft vacation leave programs in a way that encourages their use, and leadership needs to send appropriate signals that time for life is important and is not antithetical to career progression.

» Many employees in the "sandwich (or panini) generation" face both child care and elder care responsibilities, and Whole-Person employers can help alleviate their stress. Employers can help these employees by investing in elder care supports, providing informational assistance, and allowing time for family care.

» Many employees have the desire but lack the time to volunteer for charitable causes. Employers can help employees by providing PTO for volunteering, holding company charity events, and even involving employees' families in philanthropy. By doing so, you are supporting your employees' priorities and building your cultural values around community service.

» Employees must embrace lifelong learning in order to keep up in a dynamic business environment. You can support learning through direct educational assistance and tuition programs.

» In addition, helping employees develop through specialized certificate programs or in-house learning options help upskill your workforce and show your concern for their personal and professional growth.

» 401k and other retirement investment plans enable your employees to save for their futures. Employers can help through corporate matches and by extending these benefits to employees at every wage level.

» Recent college graduates are often saddled with crippling student loan debt. By helping these employees with loan repayment, you can help alleviate a major stressor in their lives, generating engagement and loyalty.

» Finally, some employers go so far to help pay for employee weddings and for the tuition of employees' children. While these may be beyond your means, there are many creative ways to provide financial assistance to help employees through major life events.

» Every employee is unique. This means Whole-Person employers need to offer a wide range of supports, listen to employee concerns, and create custom solutions that make sense for our workforce.

CHAPTER 6 – EMBEDDING WHOLE-PERSON WORKPLACE VALUES INTO EMPLOYEE SELECTION, ONBOARDING, AND WORK DESIGN

THIS IS MY FAVORITE QUOTE about marriage, from Dr. Joyce Brothers[1]:

Marriage is not just spiritual communion. It is also remembering to take out the trash.

I love this quote because it gets to the heart of it. Yes, marriage is about romantic love, but more importantly it is about doing right by the person you love by doing the mundane, often thankless tasks that make their life better.

Similarly, having Whole-Person Workplace values is one thing, but you also need to "remember to take out the trash"- take care of the typical slate of day-to-day managerial and HR activities in a way that expresses these values. In fact, these seemingly mundane activities may be even more important that policies and programs that are expressly constructed to be "family friendly" or "whole-person".

These next two chapters are a little different from the rest of the book, which to this point, has emphasized the need to do new, more, or different things to become a Whole-Person Workplace. In this chapter, we're going to discuss how we can embed Whole-Person Workplace values into how we hire new employees, onboard them, and design work. In Chapter 7, we'll cover embedding these values into how we evaluate performance and provide pay and benefits.

BUILDING A WHOLE-PERSON WORKPLACE THROUGH EMPLOYEE SELECTION

So far in this book, we've described the need for leaders, managers, and the HR department to embody Whole-Person values. However, organizations are not just a function of leader behavior. Everyone can contribute to creating and sustaining a supportive workplace.

In fact, several leaders I interviewed made the important point that employer support for employees needs to be matched by employee commitment. For example, Danielle DeBoer of Novartis said, "There are two sides to it- The responsibility of the employer to support employees, but also the responsibility of the employee to reciprocate." Chris Geschickter, CHRO at Johnstone Supply, added, "It's a two-way relationship. If you go above and beyond for an employee, it comes back to you. If employees go above and beyond for you, it comes back to them. Freedom, flexibility and responsibility flows both ways." The first way to ensure reciprocity is by hiring people who will appreciate your values.

Going further, you want to make sure you hire people into your organization who reflect and can help you grow your Whole-Person values. For example, I was recently speaking with a former student of mine, who is now a rising star in HR at ADP. She told me of a prior employer and how, after Hurricane Sandy ravaged the New Jersey coast, "employees took it upon ourselves to help each other by pooling their unused paid days off and giving them to colleagues who were left without power, access to work, or were dealing with even tougher things like losing homes or having to care for family."

What she describes is called a Leave Donation or Leave-Sharing Program[2]. In programs like these, employees can give some of their accumulated paid time off to their coworkers- most typically to help them through a medical emergency or, in this case, in the aftermath of a natural disaster. What a wonderful example of colleagues stepping up to help colleagues. This is the type of attitude that builds Whole-Person Workplaces, not just from the top-down, but also peer-to-peer.

Hiring for Culture Fit

When we hire employees, we err if we only focus on qualifications and skills. Obviously, these are important, but you also would be wise to consider the importance of culture-person fit, fit with your core company values, some important personality traits, and whether the new hire is aligned with Whole-Person Workplace values.

For example, online retailer Zappos.com is known as a pro-employee workplace with a collaborative, non-hierarchical culture built on everyone bringing their "whole selves to work." When they hire, they typically conduct two sets of interviews. The first set is focused on work experiences, technical skills, and track record. The second is focused on personality and culture fit. Applicants have to do well in both to be hired. As founder and CEO Tony Hsieh explained, "We've passed on lots of smart and talented people who we know could have an immediate impact on our top or bottom line. But if they're not a culture fit, we just won't hire them. And the reverse is true, we'll fire people if they're not good for the culture, even if they are doing their work perfectly fine.[3]" This is particularly important at Zappos, as one employee cheerfully states, "because it's all up to everyone to grow this culture.[4]"

Similarly, SAS, a leading statistical software company widely recognized as a best place to work, declares, "highly productive jerks and lone wolves don't work here, they just won't get the culture." At Southwest Airlines, founder and former CEO Herb Kelleher famously said, "We will hire someone with less experience, less education and less expertise rather than someone who has more of those things and has a rotten attitude. Because we can train people. You can't pull this off the other way around- can you imagine an airline trying to hire experienced flight attendants and then training them to be funny?[5]"

Johnstone Supply is a much smaller company, with 140 or so employees- but they also are committed to hiring for fit with their core values, which center on excellence in customer service. CHRO Chris Geschickter at Johnstone Supply told me that:

> We are a family-owned company- the founders started the company because they wanted contractors to get a better customer experience- and we have a very family feel. When I was hired 2 years ago, I didn't have to sell them on the importance of core values and managing towards them. They already knew and promoted this. It's how we hire and keep employees.

New Moon Natural Foods also reinforces its culture by hiring for culture fit. According to founder and president, Billy Griffin:

> We were founded as a values-based organization around ethical and sustainable food. And we tend to attract people with these values. Our workplace values are similar- diversity, fairness, tolerance, and mutual support.
>
> When I initially talked with our HR supervisor- who by the way started for us punching a register- about how we wanted to interview, I described it this way: 'You're throwing a party. Who are you inviting? Would you invite someone to a party that wouldn't get along with the other guests? Or someone who was exactly the same as everyone else? That doesn't make for a great party.' We want to hire people whose values fit our Whole-Person culture.
>
> If we fail to hire someone with our cultural values, it becomes apparent very quickly, and our team will step up to enforce our values- either the new employee catches on, or they don't stay too long. Because we hire well, we in management don't have to enforce the culture because it becomes something we all craft together.

Hiring for Personality Fit

Aside from qualifications and skills, as well as culture and core values, it is also important to select employees based on some important personality styles that research has linked to higher levels of engagement, agility, and cultural success. These qualities are most consistent with building and maintaining a Whole-Person Workplace.

One important quality to look for is growth mindset, a concept defined and popularized, initially in the field of educational psychology, by Carol Dweck[6]. People with growth mindsets believe that their traits are not fixed- they can improve, acquire new skills, and gain new understandings. As a result, they tend to see failure as a growth opportunity, while rejecting zero-sum thinking (i.e., if someone is winning, someone else, like me, is losing). By contrast, people with a fixed mindset tend to emphasize the possible downsides and threats that change can bring and, as a result, usually resist change.

By hiring those with growth mindsets to your company, you engender a positive, adaptable atmosphere. Employees with growth mindsets are more likely to help others in their workplace and see support for colleagues (like new parents) as a good thing, not as a loss for them. Those with growth mindsets are better able to receive constructive feedback and work towards career development goals.

You can ask specific types of behavioral interview questions to assess mindset[7], such as "In your previous role, what was the biggest mistake you made, and what did you learn from it?" Someone giving a growth-mindset-answer would be honest about their mistake, what they learned, and how they improved as a result.

Similarly, employees with high emotional intelligence (EQ) can be assets to Whole-Person Workplaces. People with high EQ tend to be aware of, control, and express their emotions, and are able to handle interpersonal relationships judiciously and empathetically[8]. Obviously, empathy and interpersonal skill are very important for providing emotional and tangible support to coworkers and those one supervises. EQ allows people to understand others' situations and work with them on solutions- the very actions that help you craft a Whole-Person culture.

As with growth mindset, you can use behavioral interviews to assess EQ[9], with questions like, "Tell me about a time when you neutralized a stressful situation," or "Tell me about a time when you had to work cohesively as a team with people you didn't like[10]."

Hiring for Whole-Company Values

Finally, you can directly discuss Whole-Person Workplace values during the hiring process. Before I hire someone, I'd want to know if they are looking for a place where they can bring their whole selves to work. I'd want to know what their orientation is to supporting their fellow employees through their life and family challenges- and whether they've had experience doing so. I'd want to know if they agree with, will uphold, and will help promote values at your company. Finally, I'd like to see if they have the potential to become a leader who would take a Whole-Person approach in how they support and manage their employees.

Building a true Whole-Person Workplace requires everyone to be involved. After all, leave donation programs don't just organize themselves.

EMPLOYEE ONBOARDING

As we discussed in Chapters 1 and 2 on Covid and flexibility, the shift to remote work has led many workplaces to become far more intentional about how they communicate and handle highly interpersonal situations. This intentionality is particularly important for employee orientation- whether this is done face-to-face in an actual workplace or remotely with lots of Zoom calls.

Recall how Brie Reynolds described the employee orientation at Flexjobs, which has been a fully remote workforce for 14 years:

In terms of orienting new hires in this environment, we recently brought 5 on board. After, one of them said our onboarding process was better than any in-person orientation they experienced before. At his last company, he wasn't onboarded at all, just brought to his cubicle, and "oh, right... we forgot to order you a computer." How is an employee going to make sure they deal with all the details if the company doesn't?

It helps a new employee so much if you can give structure to their initial days, make them feel part of real team, and see how everything works together. We set up individual meeting times for them to learn about the whole company. For the first two weeks, they spend about 2-3 hours a day meeting with teammates and attending trainings. We set up follow-up check-in times, so we can really show them what their worklife will be like.

Similarly, a friend of mine was recently hired during remote-working times at Merck, and he echoed many of the same sentiments- that his online and Zoom-based onboarding and orientation were better than the in-person ones he'd experienced before. He told me, "they really took the time to train, to help me understand the whole process and who I'd be connecting with. They took their time making me part of the team before having me dive into work."

A proper employee onboarding needs to accomplish several important things. First, the new employee needs to be situated in their job- understand their tasks, roles and responsibilities. Also, orientation needs to cover important legal and HR issues, such as harassment law and workplace safety. Further, new employees have to be guided through the logistics of the workplace- paperwork, ID badges, tech, passwords, access to information. This is sometimes overlooked, but as CPLL's Amy Beacom reminded us in Chapter 3, "the procedural pieces can derail an entire experience." No matter how well you design orientation, if the new employee can't get their parking pass, their first impression of your workplace is torpedoed.

Orienting New Employees to Whole-Person Values

However, onboarding should be much more- it should introduce new employees to your core values and culture. For example, at Zappos, new employees get two week's orientation to company culture. Then, as customer service is one of their core values, all employees, regardless of their position, go through two week's customer service training. Only after this training, do they go on to their job and job-specific training[11]. Great companies have been imbuing their onboarding with core company values for a long time. Dan Domenench of HPE recalls an early career experience at Allied Signal in the 1990s when legendary CEO Larry Bossidy[12] exhorted new hires about the importance of work-family balance during orientation.

Onboarding should also help a new employee meet a wide variety of their coworkers, generating an internal network of people who can help them learn more about the company and its culture, get up and running at their job, and support their ongoing development.

At a recent professional development event for my undergraduate business students, alumni Robert Russo of Bristol-Myers Squibb gave my students great advice on how to manage their first few weeks after being hired. He advised the students to, "approach their supervisor and ask her for a list of 10 people who would be helpful to meet while they are getting established." Great advice- but a Whole-Person Workplace shouldn't put that responsibility on the new employee. Rather, supervisors or those running orientations should take it upon themselves to identify current employees who are best positioned and inclined to provide both instrumental and social support to a new hire.

In his book, *The Best Place to Work*[13], author and consultant Ron Freidman notes that many companies don't sufficiently prioritize the human side of their workplace, especially during onboarding. He advocates that one of the most important goals of onboarding is to help a new employee make connections that can develop into significant relationships- such as mentors, "best work friends," and friendships that extend outside of work. Friedman discusses Gallup's now famous insight that the employee survey question that is most predictive of engagement and performance at work is, "Do I have a best friend at work?[14]" Not pay, or working conditions, but a human connection.

There are many things we can do to foster friendly relationships at work, and Friedman suggests stretching out the process, so that a new employee can have meaningful one-on-one or small group meet-and-greets over a period of time, instead of a flood of back-to-back-to-back rushed meetings.

Recognizing New Employees as Whole People

Whole-Person Workplaces should also recognize the whole person right from the start. *The Best Place to Work* also provides examples of companies that extend their welcome to a new employee's family. For instance, McMurray, a marketing agency, sends cookies to a new hire's house to celebrate the job acceptance; Talent Plus, a recruitment firm, invites the new employee's family for a tour of the workplace. Lisa Evans, the director of talent development at Conagra Foods- the company behind such brands as Birdseye and Chef Boyardee- told me about how they involve employees' families:

> *We make food, so our employees' work is very tangible, so it's fun to pull kids into. Every so often, we have days where we invite the families for a full day of activities- get the kids cooking recipes with our foods and everything. This gets them excited about what their parents do, and it connects and adds meaning for our employees. It really speaks to our culture and employee engagement. Employers aren't a number- we recognize them as a person, a parent.*

Workplaces could also ask about new employees' social activities or charities they support and put respect on these through gestures, donations, or other recognition- for example, sponsoring an employee's kid's youth soccer team, matching charitable contributions, or hosting a fund-raiser. If a new employee is involved in their local community theater, you could donate to that theater or, better yet, make sure lots of employees and leaders attend their shows. Ginny Kissling of Ryan, LLC told me that, "On Veterans Day, any veteran or spouse of a veteran gets that day off, as a way to recognize and honor that aspect of them as a person."

Tom Prendergast of Jugtown Country Store sums up the importance of respecting employees as whole people, "Trying to be a good person shouldn't be as hard as some make it out to be. Treat people like people, and realize that little things aren't little things. Even something like remembering and celebrating someone's birthday recognizes them as people."

In one awesome example, a company I know acknowledged a new hire by finding out where her co-ed softball team had after-game drinks and picked up the bill for that new employee and her team.

If you take the time to get to know your employees' priorities, and then think creatively about recognizing them, there are almost infinite ways to signal sincere interest in your new employees as whole people.

REASSESSING WORK DESIGN FOR FLEXIBILITY

As we discussed in detail in Chapter 2, workplace flexibility is perhaps the most important way we can support employees with their life challenges. Flexibility gives employees the time and space they need to develop solutions that work for the specific contours of the challenges they face. There are several things we can do to enhance possibilities for flexible work[15].

First, we can analyze the work to be done and break it into component parts. By doing so, you'll likely find that many tasks, even those that are not obvious candidates for being done flexibly, lend themselves to alternative approaches. This is the logic behind State Street's award-winning manager-initiated flex program[16]. In this program, managers are responsible for periodically examining the jobs they supervise to uncover parts of the work can be done more flexibly. Managers then approach their employees to present the range of options available, often including flextime, telework, compressed schedules, and job sharing. As a result, their internal surveys show that expanded work options led to greater employee engagement and reduced turnover.

Next, as also mentioned in Chapter 2, we can also uncover opportunities for more flexible work by considering how the work of employees fit together and finding ways to increase work substitutability. For instance, by developing a team around an important client or project, you take the onus off of a single employee to be solely responsible while feeling pressured to be "always available." Of course, more substitutable work requires excellent communication and effective use of available coordination technologies.

These approaches also promote development of junior employees, who can learn from more senior mentors, and create flexibility for when employees take vacation, parental leave, or other time off. Recall what Bill Plastine at BASF said about his work group and how it enabled him to take his parental leave with a clear conscience and feeling well-supported:

> *The type of work we do in employee development is very collaborative and mostly involves long-term projects. In my area, we build teams in a way so people can jump in and out as needed. We always had enough people knowledgeable about a project to keep it running well. And those who take leave can easily pick up where we leave off. We also cross-train between projects, so we have flexibility. For example, for our onboarding program, there's not just one person involved. There's someone who owns it, but many well-versed in it so we can work as an interconnected team. I think this is a smart approach to work design that existed*

before leave policies, but this approach and culture works really well for these situations.

REASSESSING WORK DESIGN FOR EMPLOYEE MOTIVATION

While the new trend to work-from-home and flexible work is certainly front of mind, let's not forget some of the classic approaches to designing work for high intrinsic motivation- that is, work that is more conducive to high levels of engagement, satisfaction, and performance. This is a key component of building a Whole-Person Workplace for all our employees, including essential workers and those who can't work flexibly.

In their classic Job Characteristics Model[17], Hackman and Oldham uncovered elements of work (independent of pay or rewards) that lend themselves to high motivation. In essence, they found that work is more satisfying and motivating when employees[18]:

» Perform a variety of tasks and demonstrate a variety of skills on the job

» Can see an entire project or piece of work through from beginning to end

» Understand how their work positively impacts others

» Are given autonomy over where, when, and how one can do their work

» Receive feedback to track their performance and development

One important part of this model is that the implications extend to employees in all types of work. Even if essential employees can't work remotely, you can add skill variety and developmental feedback to their work, resulting in higher engagement.

Can you think of ways to demonstrate how important someone's work is to customers or to internal clients? To get back-of-house employees to meet the customers that their work has helped? Can we cross-train and rotate employees, so they are constantly learning and newly challenged? Can we give retail employees more autonomy over how their work gets done, while delegating authority to them to make certain decisions? Can a warehouse or factory employee see how their work contributes to the whole? Perhaps teams can self-manage, seeing things through from end to end and feeling more empowered? If you take the time to consider these factors, any number of work design interventions become possible.

Daniel Pink built on the Hackman and Oldham framework by emphasizing autonomy, mastery, and purpose as the key drivers for person-enhancing work[19]. Pink's approach helps uncover ways to add developmental opportunities to jobs, helping employees gain the satisfaction of building mastery. He also emphasizes connecting the profit motive to a higher purpose[20]. For example, those managing mortgage loan officers should emphasize the important purpose of their department's work- helping families reach their American dream of home ownership-rather than just the profit motive of generating fees and revenue.

Similarly, psychologist Adam Grant conducted an experiment with employees who solicited donations from a university's alumni. He found that motivation, engagement, performance, and results soared after employees met with students who received scholarships and other opportunities because of alumni donations[21]. Understanding purpose leads to better work, higher motivation, and better employee experiences.

CAPACITY MANAGEMENT AND COMBATTING CHRONIC OVERWORK

Another important aspect to work redesign is what ThirdPath Institute's Jessica DeGroot calls "human capacity management." That is, many employees who work flexibly often work harder, longer hours than before. If this pressure continues for too long, it results in chronic overwork[22], which crushes engagement, satisfaction, and performance, and also leads to negative mental and physical health outcomes[23]. DeGroot offers an important analogy of a glass of water always filled to the brim, "If there's any additional shock to the system, a last-minute emergency, it results in overflow- there's no more capacity to deal with the unexpected."

Sometimes, people do this to themselves, but often, employers are complicit in failing to ensure boundaries between work and life, even if work is being done from home. Danielle DeBoer of Novartis observes, "Some research shows people are working more hours [now that we're working from home]. 40 hours turned into 50 then 60, and will this now be the expectation?"

In a recent but pre-Covid Families and Work Institute study[24], one third of employees reported chronic overwork, citing more than one of the following causes:

» Extreme job demands, in that they are given more work than can be reasonably accomplished even in 50-60 hour workweeks

» Expectations that they stay connected to work remotely (emails, calls, texts) after work hours

» The inability to avoid "low value-added" tasks, such as paperwork or unnecessary meetings

» Having too many projects to work on at one time, diminishing their ability to focus and prioritize among projects and creating too many interruptions and distractions

Even within reasonable working hours, it is important to respect people's time while at work. According to a Staples.com survey[25], more than a third of office employees say they are victims of email overload, one in five report they spend more than two hours a day in meetings, and over a quarter characterize the meetings they attend as inefficient. Zoom meeting fatigue is a very real, more current problem- as Beth Rivera of Uncommon Goods notes, "Almost every call is a zoom call. On video all day long your eyes start to hurt." The Covid approach to remote work has taught us that we need to be more intentional about our communication, and we should redouble these efforts when it comes to emails and meetings, whether work is in-person or remote.

Even if work hours are long, workers experience less burnout if they are given chances throughout the day to recharge and refocus. It's when employees feel compelled to press on through lunch and forego breaks that they hit their physical and psychological limits. Meanwhile, workers who modulate the pace of their work and occasionally step away from it, often literally by taking a walk, experience overall boosts in productivity[26].

Managers can role model and support the need for these small breaks, for example with group lunches, a make-over for the employee lounge, or setting aside time for coffee chats. In fact, some employers schedule a mid-afternoon 15-minute "recess" for all employees to take a break at the same time[27] (no word if they use that time to play on the swing set). What a great idea to encourage the use of break time and encourage social interaction.

Examples of Whole-Person Approaches to Capacity Management

It is especially important that, when the boundaries between home and work have been eroded, Whole-Person workplaces help employees avoid chronic overwork and maintain healthy work lives. Thankfully, some have developed ways to do this.

For example, Volkswagen was among the first to shut down its email for all but emergency messages after hours[28], and now many companies (and even entire European countries[29]) have followed suit. Cynthia Calvert of Workforce 21C is a fan of such policies:

> One policy I like is not checking email after certain times, and not checking communication after hours except in an emergency. People want to prove worth by appearing busy- and that spreads to everyone else needing to seem busy. Especially when you work from home, it's harder to have those boundaries. You're grateful for your job and want to prove your worth.

Karen Cardona, culture manager at Convene, a hospitality and events management company, appreciates that, "we shut down operations and emails on weekends, even for client-facing employees. The founders believe it is important to separate from work on weekends, recharge and not get burned out- of course, unless there is a weekend event we're working, but we have a lot of notice for things like that."

Further, my friend who was successfully onboarded remotely at Merck also observed that they have a healthy attitude towards avoiding chronic overwork, "during orientation, they flat-out told me that if I find myself working more than 40-45 hours a week, to let us know, and we'll cycle some things off your plate for a while. Because they've been running with this culture for a long time, it's just how they operate."

Famously, the Boston Consulting Group, long known for its "work-first" culture, implemented their Red Zone program to combat chronic overwork[30]. This program identifies employees whose work hours could lead to burnout and temporarily reduces their workloads. After initial resistance from employees, Red Zone has become a successful program that has helped with recruitment, retention, and reputation.

But what follows is my favorite example because, at this firm, human capacity management is fully integrated into the business model.

Typically, law firms are notorious for chronic overwork- in part owing to their billable hours model for compensation and promotion. Most firms require at least 2000 billable hours a year. However, Applegate & Thorne-Thomsen[31], a Chicago-based law firm, bucks that trend by setting billable hours goals for full-time associates at 1700 hours and embracing part-time and flexible work for many employees.

According to founder Ben Applegate, "I make sure that the clients know at the outset that they can't schedule a regular weekly conference call on the day he or she is off. If the person works a flex schedule and leaves at 1:30, 2:00, 3:00, we don't schedule conference calls in the late afternoon. I think most clients are pretty understanding." The firm also sells clients on the fact that they have extra capacity to handle last-minute emergencies if they come up, "Because my lawyers aren't chronically overworked, they have the capacity- in terms of time, energy, and mental focus- to respond effectively to crisis situations. We can rise to these occasional challenges because we don't treat every day like a crisis[32]."

Their approach is also a competitive advantage for recruitment and retention. Despite offering salaries 15-20% below market, they have their pick of hires from elite law schools and those who burned out at other firms, because "even lawyers want to enjoy a life outside of work." Applegate adds, "people see the value proposition for working 300 hours less for a little bit less money." Being a Whole-Person Workplace enabled this firm to achieve a sustainable competitive advantage, as well as manage their firm according to their core values, countering the industry trend towards chronic overwork and creating a more humane environment for their employees.

Role-Modeling to Discourage Overwork

It is important that leaders not only support healthy work-life balance, but that they emulate and role-model balance themselves. For example, Dan Domenech recalls a time when, while he was at Dun & Bradstreet, he witnessed this type of leadership:

> We were at a meeting and a junior HR leader told us she was taking some vacation time but that 'she'd be available.' Our boss said, 'No, you will not be available, you are on vacation! We've got you covered.' Whoa! I never had a boss who said that before. That's true leadership. Later on that summer was maybe the first time in my career I did not check in during vacation.

Amy Beacom of CPLL shares a similar story:

> You need to walk your talk and provide the support when needed, and leaders especially need to be visible doing these things themselves.

> A new mom who was just returning from parental leave told her boss that her goal was to be out by 5pm, so that even with her commute, she can have some family time after work. She started going home at 5, but it slowly kept creeping later, and by second

week, she backslid to leaving at 6pm. Her boss was a dad of four, knew how important family time was, and how hard it was for her to leave as she was a perfectionist. So, the supervisor started coming to her desk at 5pm, with his own briefcase and jacket, and told her it's time for them to leave. That's visible leadership- showing how important this time is and supporting it in front of everyone.

I don't know about you, but I aspire to be that kind of role model and to create workplaces where employees are supported as whole people and in their lives outside of work.

THE FINAL WORD

We can plant the seeds for a Whole-Person Workplace by paying attention to some of the employee-related functions we are already engaged in. By taking the extra step of ensuring that our Whole-Person values come through in how we hire employees, how we welcome them into our company, how we design workflow, and how we combat the gravitational pull of chronic overwork, we are doing the important, sometimes mundane, everyday work to ensure a great workplace for everyone.

When we pay attention to these details, we follow the sage advice of Dr. Joyce Brothers- we don't just say we care about employees; we demonstrate that care by putting in the work. Just like all the good spouses out there who remember to take out the trash.

THOUGHTS AND ADVICE

» Building a Whole-Person Workplace isn't just about new family-friendly programs, it also involves embedding your values into everyday employee management.

» Hiring people who fit with, and can help you build upon, your workplace values is a force multiplier- it can accelerate your development as a Whole-Person Workplace. Culture is not solely determined by leadership, but is also propagated by employees willing to contribute.

» Make sure your selection criteria include whether job candidates fit with your company values and the culture you are trying to create. Also, personality factors, such as growth mindset and emotional intelligence, are consistent with Whole-Person values and should be a factor in your hiring process.

» Employee onboarding is not just about job training and policy manuals- onboarding should also welcome the whole person to your workplace. You can do this by spending time orienting new hires to your culture and values, while helping them build an internal network of colleagues happy to befriend them.

» Consider validating aspects of your new employees' lives outside work with sincere gestures of support when they first come on board.

» We can uncover opportunities for more flexible work by considering jobs, people, and culture. Further, by redesigning work flow around teams and collaboration, we can create more substitutable work, enabling employees to better manage their time and avoid overwork.

» We should examine the jobs in our areas to see if there are opportunities to add skill variety, task significance, autonomy, and developmental feedback into the work itself. These factors are particularly important for essential work that may not be amenable to flex.

» Most of us are motivated by opportunities for autonomy, mastery, and purpose. We can enhance productivity and employee satisfaction by tapping into these motivators.

» Human capacity management means setting reasonable expectations for work hours, performance, and time off, so we don't burn out our employees. Many companies have found ways to counteract the pressure for chronic overwork, even in competitive fields like law and consulting.

» Especially as the boundaries between work and life have eroded, we need to be mindful that remote employees may be particularly susceptible to overwork.

» Respecting people's time while at work- by being more mindful about the need to send another email or call another meeting and promoting appropriate use of break time- is an important way to reduce stress and drive engagement.

» Leaders and managers need to role model appropriate boundaries and respect for priorities outside of work.

CHAPTER 7 – EMBEDDING WHOLE-PERSON WORKPLACE VALUES INTO PERFORMANCE EVALUATION AND TOTAL COMPENSATION

"Is anyone else freaking out right now?" Dan Price asked after the clapping and whooping died down into a few moments of stunned silence. "I'm kind of freaking out.[1]"

Price, the founder and CEO of Gravity Payments, a Seattle-based credit-card processing company, took a leap of faith and fundamentally changed his firm's approach to compensation. He had just announced that, going forward, the minimum annual salary at Gravity Payments would be $70,000. No one, regardless of position, would make less. You could forgive anyone there at that moment for freaking out.

Price believed that by doing right by his employees at the most fundamental level- their paychecks- he could create a world-class workplace culture, boost performance, and, most importantly to him, enable his employees to meet their life challenges[2]. As he told CNN, "If we're actually able to pay everybody enough that they can live a normal life, then, to me, there is a moral imperative.[3]" There are many more details to this story and the positive results over the six-plus years since the announcement, and we'll get to them later on in this chapter. But first, some background.

Maslow's hierarchy of needs[4] is one of the most influential models in the history of social science. In short, Maslow proposes that people are first motivated to satisfy their most basic needs- enough money to get by, food, shelter, security. Once these needs are satisfied, social and esteem needs, such as respect, recognition, and positive relationships, become most salient. This is where many of the recommendations of this book start coming into play. Finally, only after satisfying both of those categories of needs, "higher order", more psychologically-based needs of interesting work, challenge, development, autonomy, mastery, and purpose become most important. In fact, backed by lots of research, Daniel Pink asserts that, "the best use of money as a motivator is to pay people enough so thy no longer have to think about money and can concentrate on the work.[5]"

In previous chapters, we discussed how to add psychologically rewarding elements into the design of jobs (Chapter 6) and how to enable more autonomy over where, when, and how people work (Chapter 2). This is the ideal situation- people have their "self-actualization" needs met and feel better about managing the challenges in their lives- and you get a dedicated, engaged, and productive workforce. Whole-Person Workplaces are total win-win arrangements.

In some ways, however, I've put the cart before the horse. The fact is, "higher order" rewards won't have an impact if you cannot first provide a basic foundation of job security, sufficient pay, and solid benefits. This is also the case if you can't properly assess, recognize. and provide feedback on your employee's work. Even worse, without satisfying foundational needs, attempts to address higher-order concerns come off as insincere insults. Employees are smart, and they know that being asked to work like a champ while being paid like a chump is at best disingenuous and at worst exploitative.

There's a famous quote about personal finance from James Frick[6]:

> Don't tell me where your priorities are. Show me where you spend your money and I'll tell you what they are.

While this is undoubtedly true in terms of personal spending and financial prioritization, I think it is equally, if not more, true for employers and their budgets and for leaders and their actions.

Dan Price showed his priorities. Maybe you are not ready or able to take the same leap, but I'm sure that you can devise many ways to ensure that your whole-person priorities are communicated. In this chapter, we'll discuss the most foundational aspect of the employer-employee relationship- determining the exchange of work for pay. We'll discuss how to imbue our decisions around performance evaluation and total compensation with our Whole-Person values.

UNLOCKING WHOLE-PERSON APPROACHES THROUGH PERFORMANCE EVALUATION

Whole-Person Workplaces utilize performance evaluation as a central mechanism for empowering employees and enabling flexibility. To accomplish this, we first have to do a better job measuring performance.

Common Performance Evaluation Problems and Ways to Fix Them

In many companies, managers and employees dread performance evaluations. Many managers feel uncomfortable giving feedback, and most employees feel nervous about receiving it[7]. The traditional approach to structuring performance reviews- once a year, using a stress-inducing checklist, based on hazy memory of performance, subject to lots of unintended biases[8], emphasizing "face time," "chair time," and the like- exacerbates this anxiety. Reviews become high-pressure interactions where decisions about pay, bonuses, promotions, and firings take place. Because of these negative attitudes and associations, evaluations are often not conducted in ways that promote performance, development, and better work relationships.

Even setting aside anxiety, many managers and employees complain that traditional annual performance evaluations are, at best, useless and, at worst, counterproductive. Traditional performance evaluations often represent missed opportunities to correct performance problems, develop employees, and identify top talent[9]. They demotivate employees, especially the more productive ones. These are terrible outcomes! Without doing our basic managerial functions well, we impair company performance and derail any effort to provide a Whole-Person Workplace.

Here's a quick summary of problems with traditional performance evaluations and what we can do to make them better.

First, many evaluations are conducted only once or twice a year. Because they are not done frequently enough[10], employees may not get sufficient feedback about their performance, problems don't get identified and solved until perhaps months later, and supervisors end up relying more on imperfect memories and first- and last-impressions, rather than actual performance. These impressions depend on seeing someone working, as opposed to examining their results, and are particularly ill-suited to evaluating remote or flexible workers.

Performance evaluations need to be conducted more frequently, and timing should not be based on pre-determined calendar dates, but around workflow, deadlines, and the scope of projects. Even if you retain a formal annual review for compensation or promotion decisions, you should hold regular informal feedback and coaching sessions to keep things on track. In a remote environment, you can use progress reporting, goal-setting, and weekly 10-minute Zoom calls to ensure employees get the support they need to do their best work[11] (recall Flexjob.com's "quarantine check-in template" from Chapter 2). By doing so, employees get better feedback, problems get solved more quickly, supervisors and employees develop better relationships, and the scary annual review becomes a much less pressurized event because everyone is already on the same page.

Further, many evaluations make use of a "one size fits all" approach with standardized forms and generic performance criteria[12]. As jobs and job performance can vary widely, this approach fails to capture a full picture of performance and ends up overestimating basic criteria (punctuality, quantity of work) and underestimating unique contributions. Further, the reliance upon 1-5 agree-disagree scales eliminates nuance and leads to lazy "check the boxes" thinking.

Performance evaluations should emphasize open-ended, qualitative feedback- even if some numerical scores are included. You should include detailed descriptions of effective behavior and its resulting positive outcomes, as well as ineffective behaviors and their consequences. Two people in the same job can both be very effective doing things differently; your evaluations should be able to capture this. One way to build more nuance and flexibility is to adopt a goal-setting approach[13]. With this type of review, employees and supervisors agree on performance goals for the next few months, hold periodic "check in" meetings for coaching and feedback, and finally conduct a formal review based on progress towards those specific goals. This approach is also effective in remote-working environments.

Another limitation of performance appraisals is that, most commonly, evaluations are conducted only by one's supervisor. While theirs is a valuable perspective, it is only one subjective point of view- ignoring more objective data and the perspectives of peers, customers, or a wider range of 360-degree feedback[14]. Specific work outcomes, metrics, and employee self-evaluations should be included in order to ensure a fuller picture of performance.

But there is hope. Over the past decade, many companies have adopted new and more innovative approaches to performance evaluation-focused on goal-setting, frequent employee-supervisor "check-ins," input from peers, and the use of app-based technology to provide frequent performance updates and feedback[15]. Here are just a few of many examples.

Examples of Companies Conducting Better Performance Evaluations

At Deloitte,[16] the heart of performance evaluations for auditing teams is a focus on peer feedback, timed around their project work together. The Gap[17], with its mostly hourly retail workforce, has traded in generic rating scales for nuanced evaluations based on broad goal attainment. They focus on monthly "touch points"- developmental conversations between employees and supervisors- instead of formal annual reviews. In both of these cases, the new systems have resulted in increased satisfaction for both employees and managers, as well as a reduction in time, cost, and paperwork- opening up more time for valued-added work.

In the 1970's, General Electric pioneered the traditional, strict approach to annual performance evaluations. Famously, through their forced distribution program, managers could only identify a relatively small percentage of employees as excellent and had to identify their bottom 10% or so of performers. The first group were fast-tracked for raises and promotions; the latter group were let go, and the remaining 70% received comparatively little attention. At the time, GE justified this approach to jump-start their company out of a low-performance culture- former CEO Jack Welsh explained, "Managers weren't giving employees candid feedback. Every rating was always satisfactory." Unfortunately, this approach, after serving its purpose for a time, led to intense internal competition and jockeying for favor- especially in the month or so leading up to reviews.

Today, GE uses an innovative app-based system called PD@GE[18]. This app allows employees to continuously share performance milestones with their teams and managers, managers to provide frequent feedback through performance "touchpoints" to employees, and peers to provide real-time developmental feedback and recognition. The new approach has focused employees and managers on continuous improvement and development, rather than competition. Decisions on raises, promotions, and developmental opportunities now occur year-round, as opposed to just after competitive reviews. After all, as GE's CHRO Susan Peters said, "The world isn't really on an annual cycle anymore for anything."

Enabling Flexibility Through Performance Evaluation

On a podcast a few years ago, I was asked to name the "most important" work-family benefit. I think they expected me to answer with parental leave or flextime. However, I replied that the most important way to support balance for employees wasn't a benefit at all. Instead, performance evaluations that focus on actual job performance, as opposed to other signifiers, such as "chair time," internal politics, or managing impressions, enable employees to work the way that best works for them and enable managers to let go of the perceived need to micromanage employees[19]. Better evaluations help us express our Whole-Person values.

Ryan, LLC, the tax firm highlighted in the introductory chapter, started from a place in which their performance reviews were antithetical to the flexible, humane, Whole-Person Workplace it is today. According to former President of Global Shared Services, Delta Emerson[20]:

> *Every year when we did talent review, the very first metric we looked at was how many hours an individual had put in during the last review period. We literally sorted that on an Excel spreadsheet... that was ingrained in our culture- people would wear their hours like badges or tattoos on their foreheads. That was a hard paradigm to break. People were focused on how much time was put in- face time and not results. You know that guilty look that you get or that you feel when somebody looks at you as you go to the elevator or if you get up from your desk it to a two o'clock? There were clock-watchers all around.*

Ryan is now a widely-recognized Results-Only Work Environment, in which employees can work from anywhere and at any time as long as their performance stays great[21]. It is now a staple on Fortune's 100 Best Places to Work For list, especially recognized for its embrace of flexibility[22].

Ryan accomplished their transformation with a constellation of changes over a decade (and with continuous improvement since), but their central intervention was its new performance evaluation system. Instead of infrequent, subjective evaluations based largely on "time on task," Ryan now has managers, employees, and teams develop a set of agreed-upon performance metrics that are consistently tracked. As long as an employee's performance along these metrics, including progress on goals, revenue generation, and internal and external customer satisfaction, are on point, they are free to work as flexibly as they need.

Again, from Delta Emerson:

It's all well and good for me to sit here and say 'when you sit down and review someone, focus on results not hours.' Now how helpful is that if you don't have something to look at? Well, fortunately we had a lot of metrics scattered around... and we were able to put a dashboard together that allows our managers and employees to see what their results are.

Every day people can log on into our intranet and see their dashboard. If they're revenue producing, it has their revenue targets- what their benchmark is, what they've achieved, where they stand, and what percentage they've got tied to that. If they are non-revenue producing, they have goals that are incentive based, and it shows them where they stand on their goals. Also client satisfaction ratings.... Managers get one more layer of evaluation. We track turnover and engagement scores in their groups- holding managers accountable for managing employees, coupled with incentives.

This system was a gift that we gave to all of our managers so that they can become more effective in this environment. That, combined with the ability to have intelligent conversations on performance, has been incredibly helpful. Work can now happen no matter where or when.

Once Ryan made the change, some employees who had been receiving high ratings by working 60 hour weeks were revealed to have been less productive than others who worked fewer but more efficient hours. Turnover plummeted; satisfaction, engagement, and financial performance soared, and this success continues today.

Embedding Whole-Person Values Through Performance Evaluation

Ryan's experience provides evidence that the best thing managers and employers can do for all their employees- and especially those facing work-family conflict- is to do the hard work of actually evaluating performance, not chair time or face time. When managers do this, they free employees to arrange their work and family lives.

As Doreen Anthony of Concord Health puts it, "There's no greater gift than time"- especially when employees can use that time to create custom-fit solutions for the many challenges they face outside of work. In my opinion, allowing for flexibility through better performance management may be the purest expression of Whole-Person Workplace values.

Perhaps some firms can't transform the way Ryan did, certainly not in the short run. But many necessary changes don't require a full-scale overhaul of your company's performance management system. In fact, there are several small modifications that individual managers can make on their own[23]. Think about how much more competitive your whole organization would be and how much more we can express our Whole-Person values, if we:

» Defined performance in terms of customer satisfaction, core activities, or project completion.

» Regularly held goal-setting and feedback sessions with employees, and used goal attainment as the core of performance evaluation.

» Understood which aspects of employees' jobs lend themselves to flexible work and which need to be performed at set times in the office.

» Allowed more flexibility in how, when, and where work gets done, while ensuring that enough time is spent at the office to promote communication, collaboration, and innovation.

» Gradually allowed more freedom and flexibility for employees who perform well and earn trust.

» Recognized that we can maintain or even increase performance standards in professional environments while letting go of how work gets done.

By implementing some of these changes, we allow all employees to construct schedules that work best for their success at work and at home. This obviously benefits working parents who juggle work and home. But all employees gain by being able to use their time flexibly, and employers gain in terms of engagement and performance.

Ryan isn't the only company that has figured out how to embed their values into their performance evaluation system. Remember the Zappos example from last chapter- not only do they hire people based on both qualifications and culture fit, they also evaluate employees based on both on performance and "whether they are living and promoting Zappos culture.[24]" Similarly, the performance evaluation program at Johnstone Supply places its values front and center. CHRO Chris Geschickter:

When we do performance reviews, our values are our leading criteria. In fact, the majority of how we do performance evaluation is by reflecting on our core values- and then assessing whether an employee's behavior is aligned with them- in terms of customer service, teamwork, and such. We really drill down to describing behavior aligned with these core values. What does behavior that is an excellent representation of our values look like? What's a good representation? What isn't satisfactory? These behavioral examples are really helpful. To us, performance evaluation is a conversation throughout the year, and a lot of self-evaluations.

Fixing your performance evaluations is good for you as an employer. If done right, evaluations can help employees develop, feel recognized, and do better work. It helps you make better decisions about pay and career tracks. Most importantly, good performance evaluations can also help you reinforce your company values and enable your employees to work in more flexible ways.

EXPRESSING WHOLE-PERSON VALUES THROUGH TOTAL COMPENSATION

Every company has its own pay strategy. From a competitive point of view, many employers try to keep wages down (for all but executives) and see this as a win for shareholders. While this approach may make short-term economic sense, there are many employers who understand that paying good wages is a more humane and sustainable long-term strategy. For employers, pay structure is a direct reflection of values- like Frick says, "Don't tell me where your priorities are. Show me where you spend your money, and I'll tell you what they are."

Paying a Livable Wage

There are many examples of companies in typically lower-paying industries who buck that trend. For example, in the supermarket industry, both Trader Joe's and Whole Foods are known for providing higher-than-industry wages. At Trader Joe's, even a decade ago, full-time employees started at about $41,000 a year, with $950 in annual bonuses and $6,300 in retirement contributions[25]. Their average annual pay increase is 10%, and store managers can make up to $132,000.[26] Similarly, Whole Foods offers a $15 minimum wage and an average hourly rate of just over $20. Despite some turbulence after their acquisition by Amazon, they still offer some of the best pay and benefits in the industry[27]. Whole Foods also believes in pay transparency, and any employee can see the pay of any other employee, including top management's[28]. This transparency fits with their egalitarian culture and has been helpful in reducing potential gender-based wage gaps.

Similarly, The Container Store pays entry level wages 50-100% higher than their local competitors, along with cross-training, opportunities for growth, and good benefits- including health insurance for all employees, even part-timers. Their turnover is a quarter of the industry average, and they receive so many applications they can be very choosy in selecting quality employees who fit their team-based culture[29]. For a retailer with a largely hourly workforce to have been twice named overall #1 on Fortune's 100 Best Companies to Work For list[30] proves that any employer in any industry can build a Whole-Person Workplace. (Incidentally, Whole Foods and The Container Store are two of a very small group of companies to have made the list in at least 17 consecutive years.)

Shake Shack offers cashiers an average starting hourly rate of $14.80, about 40% above industry averages, and advocates for higher minimum wage laws[31]. Among big-box retailers, Costco is famous for its high wages and great health insurance benefits- even for part-time employees[32]. CNBC's Jim Cramer swears by Costco, even when other analysts feared that the wage premiums it paid during the height of the Covid pandemic would drag down their bottom line. Cramer asserted, "Costco has always paid its employees better than every other store. And it's always been a good investment because it means they can retain their best people. Chains that pay less have much higher turnover.[33]"

Yes, these employers believe their compensation strategy will generate a good return on investment through better customer service, lower turnover, and the ability to attract great employees. But they also pay living wages because of their Whole-Person values.

Two Whole-Person Examples

Uncommon Goods CEO Dave Bolotsky shares these values, both in setting his company's pay rates and as a public advocate:

> We strive to pay a living wage- we start at $18 an hour for our lowest paid worker, which is way higher than federal or New

York State minimums. We also offer generous paid time off and paid family leave.

I believe in this so much that I got involved with Time to Care New York, which successfully advocated for a higher minimum wage, paid family leave and paid sick leave in our state. We are a B-corp[34], so that got us starting to think about this issue. Then, I read into minimum wage legislation and found it horrible, that it is so low, hasn't been updated in so many years, and has become a political football. I thought this would be a conservative principle- that business should not have to rely on welfare to subsidize a poverty wage workforce. We're supposed to be opposed to government handouts- businesses should stand on their own two feet. Minimum wage should be higher and indexed to the cost of living.

You know, when you are a CEO, you are assumed to be opposed to workers' rights. Elected officials care about jobs and listen to employers, so I think when I can speak to an elected official and say we're paying a livable wage and it makes us successful, you get a good hearing and can have more impact.

Typically, the greatest benefits are offered to people who need them the least- we also need to treat our lowest paid employees with the same respect. Not just because it is good business, but it is also the right thing to do- work can be generous across the board.

Bolotsky's words almost precisely match those of Gravity Payment's Dan Price, "If we're actually able to pay everybody enough that they can live a normal life, then to me, there is a moral imperative."

Price had been talking to friends and employees who discussed the hardships of living in Seattle making $40,000 or less a year and the stress that credit-card payments, unexpected car repairs, or a trip to the emergency room could cause[35]. He also read some research on the relationship between money and happiness[36]. More money is always better, but the relationship between the two is very strong until about $70,000, then the relationship gets weaker. This makes sense- the increase in happiness going from making $25,000 a year to $50,000 a year (and all of the financial stress this would relieve), is more impactful than going from $225,000 to $250,000. That was the genesis of Gravity Payment's $70,000 minimum salary.

While Price initially wasn't trying to make a political statement (he has since become a passionate advocate[37]), his policy sent shockwaves through the business media. To most, his example was inspiring, especially because he cut his own pay from $1 million down to $70,000 as part of the program.

But others saw him as a dangerous fool. Fox Business labeled him the "lunatic of all lunatics," and Rush Limbaugh declared, "I hope this company is a case study in MBA programs on how socialism does not work, because it's going to fail.[38]" There were some initial setbacks, as several key employees quit, and his brother/co-owner sued him for failing to consult him on such a momentous decision (the suit was dismissed and Price later bought him out). But Price's biggest initial problem was that the publicity he generated left them scrambling to respond to a flood of new client inquiries.

Over time, this decision has been nothing but a boon for Gravity Payments. Revenues and profits have surged. In 2019, Gravity processed $10.2 billion in payments, more than double the $3.8 billion in 2014, before the announcement. Gravity has grown to 200 employees. Turnover is down; engagement is up.

As good as this has been for the company, it has been even better for employees[39], and in surprising ways. Employees who had been priced out of good apartments and starter homes were able to buy. Employees joined local gyms. One employee could finally afford the $400 plane ticket to visit her family in Arkansas. Some moved closer to work and started commuting by bike. But what really caught my eye was that, in the 21 months after the initial announcement, ten Gravity employees had newborn children, and two more were expecting[40]. In 2015, one new dad said, "The newfound financial stability really helped us make that decision that now would be a good time to start a family, Because of it, also, my wife can be at home with our daughter, which is important to us."

In April 2020, when so many businesses were furloughing or laying off employees to manage budget shortfalls, Gravity Payments did something remarkable. The employees decided to take voluntary wage reductions to keep everyone employed and keep the company going through its darkest time[41]. The average voluntary pay cut was 20%; Price and the COO reduced their pay to zero. By August, Price not only ended the temporary pay reduction, but reimbursed all employees for what they had sacrificed[42].

Gravity Payments is an amazing example of how a sincere expression of Whole-Person Workplace values benefits everyone and creates a culture in which support for employees is reciprocated by employees stepping up when the employer needs them to. No reason for anyone to start freaking out.

THE FINAL WORD

When you build a Whole-Person Workplace, everyone becomes personally invested. Perhaps the most fundamental way to generate this engagement is to properly evaluate your employees' work, and then recognize their performance with a wage that enables them to rise to their life challenges.

IDEAS AND ADVICE

» Work design, challenge, and autonomy can lead to the highest levels of employee engagement. However, without meeting employees' more basic need for financial stability, employees won't be motivated and will find it harder to address their life challenges.

» You most directly demonstrate your true values to your employees by how their performance is evaluated and how they are compensated for their work.

» Traditional annual performance evaluations are often counter-productive as they cause stress, reduce motivation, and fail to develop employees with useable feedback. A wide range of companies large and small, and in many different industries, have fixed their performance evaluations over the past decade.

» Better performance evaluations are conducted more frequently, emphasize informal supervisor-employee coaching sessions, and provide detailed qualitative feedback.

» Performance evaluations can be based on goal attainment, rather than standardized rating scales, and should incorporate many different perspectives- not just the supervisor's.

» Performance criteria should be based, in part, on a clear set of company values. This promotes and reinforces employee behaviors aligned with those values.

» Excellent performance evaluations can enable managers and employees to embrace flexible work options because they focus on the quality of performance, not on how, when, and where work is performed.

» Many leading employers, even in typically low-paying industries, have developed pay strategies that help them achieve long-term success and support employees with quality wages.

» Whole-Person employers pay livable wages, well above legal minimums, not just for business purposes but because of their values. Some have become advocates for better pay and working conditions.

» When Gravity Payments enacted a $70,000 minimum salary, it gave its employees the financial stability to buy homes, invest in their health, and start families. The company flourished with greater employee engagement and retention.

» When crises hit, grateful employees step up for their employers.

CHAPTER 8 – SUPPORT FOR EMPLOYEE HEALTH AND WELLNESS

FOSTERING A PHYSICALLY AND psychologically healthy workforce is good for employees and employers. As Elizabeth Hall, Vice President of Employee Experience at Cambia Health Solutions, recommends:

We should look at the totality of well-being. We have only one body and mind, whether we are at work or at home. Wellness flows back and forth. And, of course, now with Covid, for many of us there is 100% melding of the two circles in the Venn diagram- home and work- overlapping more and more. As employers, we need to look at the totality of wellbeing options. What do our employees need for their physical and mental health, financial health, and help for caregiving? How do I help my employees be the most well they can be in all spheres in their lives?

Recognizing employees as whole people means we must pay attention to their health. After all, as Delta Emerson states, "... we get the whole person through the door. We get their backs and their hands and their minds and their hearts..."

Whole-Person Workplaces should therefore strive to support the physical and mental well-being of their employees. So much of what we've already covered in this book indirectly addresses employee wellness. For example, leave and flexibility give people the time they need to handle their life challenges. Better work design, livable wages, and core benefits can alleviate stress. Supports for parenting, caregiving, and other life priorities provide emotional benefits. And, of course, workplace safety and paid sick leave are the most direct supports of physical well-being.

In this chapter, we'll focus specifically on initiatives commonly included under the umbrella of employee wellness. First, we'll discuss how well-crafted wellness programs are a win-win for employees and employers. Next, we'll dive into specific types of supports, including health and fitness initiatives, workplace redesign, and employee assistance programs (EAPs). We'll cover ideas on crafting and promoting wellness programs that best fit your workplace and conclude with a comprehensive example of a well-constructed and strategically integrated program.

Before we dive in, we should also take note of the critical importance of wellness during the Covid pandemic[1]. For the foreseeable future, employees remain under considerable stress. Many are afraid for their health and the health of their loved ones. Some maintain an underlying fear of another economic shock and resultant income insecurity. Many may not feel comfortable working long stretches inside a shared space with many other people- even if they must in order to keep their jobs. All these factors increase the need for employer support for employee wellness.

THE CASE FOR WELLNESS PROGRAMS

Eric Williams of the NY Paid Leave Coalition is a fan of employee wellness programs:

> *Of course it is good for employees to be healthy and less stressed. Also, in terms of employers and wellness, it is hard to underestimate the gap in productivity. One's mental state is, what, 90% of your productivity? Getting a full night's sleep, taking breaks and choosing healthy habits makes a huge difference. If your employees are facing stressful life balance problems, this takes up their mental space and energy- and this is a big psychological block preventing focus and productivity. Employers should do what they can to ensure their employees feel healthy and well.*

There is evidence that wellness programs are popular with employees and return financial benefits for employers[2]. However, wellness programs' impact on employee health can vary greatly, and the accumulated research is mixed[3]. For instance, there is some evidence that those who are already healthy make the most use of wellness programs and incentives- a subsidized gym membership will be valued by someone who already works out but might not be enough to incent someone else to start.

That said, well-crafted wellness programs have been linked to many positive outcomes[4]. For employees, these benefits include weight loss, increased physical activity, success in quitting smoking, better sleep habits, healthier food choices, and increased use of gym memberships. In addition, wellness programs are linked to fewer workplace injuries and accidents, as well as increased morale. For employers, the benefits include lower health care costs, reduced absenteeism, reduced turnover, reduced workers' compensation and disability-related costs, and higher productivity. In terms of overall financial impact, Johnson & Johnson estimated that, over a six-year period, every dollar invested in their wellness program returned almost three[5].

THE WIDE RANGE OF WELLNESS PROGRAMS

Wellness programs include a wide array of options, and this variety can cause confusion. Some organizations consider almost any employee-related initiative a wellness program. For example, employee recognition, concierge laundry services, employee referral programs, donation-matching, and hybrid car incentives have been lumped together with more traditional wellness initiatives such as smoking cessation, health education, workplace fitness challenges, and on-site gyms[6].

While these are all worthy efforts, the catch-all nature of overly expansive approaches to employee wellness can hamper efforts specifically designed to improve employee health. Further, scattershot programs give the impression that they were neither well-planned nor customized to employee concerns.

This diversity of wellness programming, however, provides an opportunity. Because there are so many options, you can craft a flexible, custom-fit solution tuned specifically to the needs of your workplace. By choosing a cohesive mix of strategically integrated activities, you can create a wellness program with high impact. Here's a quick overview of benefits most often included in wellness programs[7].

Health Risk Assessments

Many companies use health risk assessments (HRAs) to determine which programs would be most important for employee health, and to foster employee participation. HRAs typically consist of surveys about lifestyle choices (smoking, stress, diet, etc.) and biometric assessments, such as blood pressure and body mass index, to help an employee better understand their health risks. Once these are determined, the employer (usually through a contracted medical professional) can provide information, resources, and invitations to programs that address those specific concerns. Some employers provide monetary incentives, often $500 off an employee's health insurance costs, to participate.

Of course, employers are required by law to protect individual health information and to ensure privacy- they should only gain access to aggregated and anonymized health information[8]. However, unless you already have a high-trust workplace, many employees may be skeptical to participate[9], and unfortunately, at many workplaces, this skepticism may be well-founded[10].

That said, the aggregated information you can get and the customized information your employees receive are important for crafting high-impact wellness programs. For example, if you have very few employees who smoke, there will be little interest and, therefore, no need to run a smoking cessation program. If you have several employees with diabetes, glucose monitors and changes to food options at work may be good investments. However, due to legitimate privacy concerns, you may want to consult with a cross-section of employees for their input before moving forward.

Support for Healthy Lifestyles

Most wellness programs provide encouragement and support for behaviors conducive to physical health[11]. Perhaps the most direct way to do this is to operate an on-site fitness center, partner with one, or subsidize gym memberships and other fitness expenses. Fitness centers provide opportunities for employees to exercise, release stress, and, in some cases, access health-related services such as massages, spin classes, and personal training. Elizabeth Hall explains the approach at Cambia Health Solutions:

> We have in-house fitness centers at our main locations. Others can get stipends to spend on health and wellness- gym memberships, equipment, even new sneakers. This gives people flexibility in how people can meet their priority for health and wellness.

Beyond fitness centers, there are a host of ways employers can promote and support healthy lifestyles. Dan Domenech of Hewlett-Packard Enterprise Solutions recalls the effective approaches to fitness he experienced at HPE and when he worked for Dun & Bradstreet:

> D&B did a great job on approaching wellness. It was a lot about the mental side- having a positive attitude, controlling what you can control, and not getting caught up in drama. They also emphasized nutrition, and framed it as being well-fueled for performance, staying hydrated- it wasn't just about weight loss. They also promoted physical recovery, rest and sleep. In fact, a 10-20 minute power nap at your desk or in a pod can make you 45% more alert the rest of your day. And they offered us a free app called Headspace for meditation.
>
> Then the part about mobility and getting moving- I really bought in. I got my Fitbit through work, and never took the

elevator again. Because of this, I take so many of my phone calls on an earpiece and walk through my calls- gotta stay moving and active. One time, I was walking by the elevator during a call, and the CEO is standing there holding the door for me, but I said, no thanks!

... My current employer is also great about this. In fact, at Hewlett-Packard, we stop work at 2pm on the second Friday of every month and employees are given that time to concentrate on their health and wellness.

Domenech's experience highlights that there are many ways to promote wellness at work. Sometimes it's providing helpful information and education. Sometimes it's buying employees fitness trackers. Sometimes it's getting people to embed healthy habits- nutrition, rest, hydration, and movement- into their workday. Sometimes it's setting aside time and giving employees freedom of choice in how they embrace wellness. And for employees who buy in, it could mean never taking the elevator again.

Hosting in-house fitness, nutrition, and lifestyle activities is another popular option. For example, an employer can bring in a sleep expert to counsel employees or a meditation guide for mindfulness training. Elizabeth Hall of Cambia describes how they've adapted their programming to make it accessible to remote workers during Covid:

We have long offered a wide-range of wellness initiatives at the workplace, but during this time of remote work... we hold webinar-based training for teams on resilience and hold online fitness classes twice a day. We have regular webinars on healthy eating with guest chef, and half-hour online yoga classes with a live instructor. During Covid, we've been more creative in our interventions to help employees stay well when their regular options may not be available.

Finally, some employers provide incentives for biking to work[12], and some go so far as to manage their own bike-sharing program or purchase bikes for interested employees. Bicycling programs can also be aligned with environmental sustainability initiatives that offer incentives for carpools and mass transit.

Healthy Food Options

In the days before we all worked at home, with our refrigerators just steps away, most employees ate at least one meal and some additional food while at work. Most of us will resume doing so when (if?) we return to the workplace. Large employers usually have a cafeteria, while others may just have a break room with a vending machine. Lots of employees bring their lunches to work, and others grab food on the go. Employers can do a lot to nudge employee diet and nutrition in a positive direction.

If you have your own cafeteria and/or contract out to a vendor to run your food service, you have a lot of control over providing healthy options[13]. For example, you can emphasize such foods as salads, whole grains, organic produce, lean meats, and healthy drinks. Further, if you identified certain health issues during your wellness HRAs, you can supplement your offerings with foods more amenable to your employee dietary restrictions- for example, gluten-free, non-dairy, and nut-free options. Some employers punctuate their healthy offerings by hosting "meatless Mondays" or other themed meals. Finally, cafeterias are great places to provide educational materials and hold workshops about nutrition and healthy food choices- people are more likely to internalize food-related messaging in food-related settings.

The cafeteria at BASF's North American headquarters provides a useful example. It is bright and open and includes seasonal access to outdoor seating. It is set up with multiple food stations, such as pasta, stir-fry, sandwiches, and flatbreads. There is an extensive salad bar in the center of the room, as well as refrigerators full of healthy drinks and grab-and-go options. Small plates and trays encourage reasonable serving sizes, and water bottle refill stations are prominent. By providing an attractive setting, healthy food options, and visual reminders of good habits, BASF demonstrates its concern for employee wellness.

Employers should also consider the food they order for meetings; it is seductively easy to default to bagels, donuts, or pizza. If you contract with a food service, you can arrange for healthy alternatives, such as wraps, salads, and fruit[14]. If you give employees food stipends for late-night work, you can encourage employees to make healthier choices by negotiating deals with preferred vendors. Employers can ensure that available vending machines contain at least some healthy options, such as non-sugary beverages and healthier snacks, such as popcorn or pretzels[15]. Finally, if you provide some free snacks in your breakroom, mix in some healthy options- if all employees have to choose from are sugars and carbs, that's what they'll wind up eating.

If you are a smaller employer or don't provide much in the way of food, you can still have an influence by providing counseling and information. Whatever your situation, you can help employees make healthier food choices while at work and in the lunches and snacks they prepare at home.

On a related note, encouraging employees to spend meal times together (of course, when it is safe to do so) is also good for employee well-being. Too many American employees eat a hurried lunch at their desks, contributing to burnout[16]. Instead, by eating in groups, employees make better use of their lunch hour and spend more time socializing with coworkers. In nice weather, employees can eat outside; walking to outdoor seating or a nearby park bench also contributes steps to one's fitness tracker's daily goal. Remote workers should be encouraged to eat lunch or take breaks over Zoom with their colleagues.

Ergonomics and Workplace Design

Employee wellness can also be integrated into how the physical work space is designed. Specifically, workspaces can be altered to reduce physical stress and to encourage movement, collaboration, flow, and connection to nature[17].

First, you should examine the ergonomics of employee work stations. In office environments, many employees sit for long stretches looking at a computer screen and performing repetitive motions, such as typing. Even though white collar work is not physically demanding, the sedentary nature of office work can contribute to stress, back pain, poor posture, eye strain, and ailments, such as carpel-tunnel syndrome.

There are creative ways to address these stressors- for example, standing and walking desks encourage movement and have been shown to reduce back and joint pain[18]. Better designed chairs, or even yoga balls, encourage better posture and core muscle development. Higher-quality computer screens can reduce glare, and enhanced keyboards can reduce repetitive stress. Of course, anything you can do to encourage employee movement- walking meetings, taking breaks, fitness trackers, going outside to eat lunch- can have an impact on employee health.

Different employees face different physical demands. Nurses, for example, are on their feet all day- why not buy them new sneakers every few months? Ditto for retail employees and food service workers. Avoiding the expenses you'd incur with just one workplace accident easily justifies the cost, plus you signal your care for often- overlooked employees. Many manufacturing and warehouse employees stand at workstations and repeatedly perform a narrow range of psychical tasks- training in proper techniques, allowing sufficient break time, and rotating employees to different workstations are ways to reduce their physical strain[19].

Of course, the physical demands of certain sectors of our workforce are quite acute[20]. While occupational safety laws are an important guide, there are many more things we can do to encourage the physical wellbeing of employees who work with their bodies. For example, lifting heavy objects obviously incurs health risks- some of which can be reduced by training employees in proper lifting techniques. Of course, simple tools, such as ramps, dollies, and handcarts, represent an important part of any solution. Injury prevention professionals and personal trainers can be brought in to help employees stay strong and flexible, reducing the chances of injury or overload. Some employers, including Loews' Home Improvement, go so far as to provide exoskeletal supports.[21] These suits ensure employees can only move in safe directions during lifting and even provide a robotic boost to make lifting easier.

In short, we should identify physical risks and work with employees on creative solutions to their specific needs.

Further, workplaces can be designed to elevate employees' mood and energy[22]. Workspaces that are cramped, dark, have lots of ambient noise, and that separate employees from each other have all been associated with lower employee morale and productivity. Conversely, physical spaces that contain natural light, live plants, communal spaces, wide hallways, open atriums, and easy access to outdoor spaces have all been associated with better employee and employer outcomes.

Workspaces can also be designed to encourage movement. For example, large, well-lit, attractive staircases are more likely to be used than out-of-the-way, dark, enclosed stairwells. Visual cues near elevators, for example, to point out where the nearest staircase is, can also be useful. Strategic placement of break rooms, conference rooms, cafeterias, and communal seating can encourage both mobility and group activity. A bright, well-stocked cafeteria with both comfortable indoor and outdoor seating will gather more employees than a dreary space in the basement. No doubt, you can make some changes yourself. However, you'll want to consult with interior designers and workplace architects for more comprehensive solutions.

Employee Assistance Programs

Many employees face stressful situations in their lives- and these challenges have become even more dire during the Covid pandemic. As a result, many employers have increasingly focused on employee mental health and, in many cases, have responded by offering or expanding upon employee assistance programs (EAP)[23], most commonly offered through outside vendors or health insurers.

EAPs offer no-cost or low-cost counseling and referral services to help employees with challenges in their non-work lives[24]. Most EAPs provide assistance on issues ranging from alcohol and substance abuse, marriage and family concerns, grief and loss, stress management, emotional distress, child and elder care pressures, and financial and legal problems. More recently, many EAPs now include an array of other services, including nurse advice lines, basic legal assistance, and adoption support. Programming now most often extends to employees' family members.

EAPs continue to add services, including, in some cases, help in finding pet-sitters and dog-walkers. Ginny Kissling of Ryan, LLC describes an unexpectedly helpful program her EAP offered:

> We contract with an EAP and, this is my favorite- there's a hotline employees can call that helps them review their medical bills, and help with troubles with Medicare payments. They helped me and my dad review his bills to make sure everything was in order- they can get so complicated with insurance and Medicare and all. This was financial help, sure, but it really was a way to eliminate stress and get me peace of mind that everything was in order and my dad was taken care of.

Starting in 2020, many EAPs offer Covid-related information and referral services, including links to county and municipal offices, school district information, and advice for self- and family-care[25].

DEVELOPING YOUR WELLNESS PROGRAM

Considering the wide range of options, it can be difficult to select the right mix of wellness programs. Chris Geschickter, CHRO of Johnstone Supply reminds us to examine our approach, "Are you really addressing their needs or just what you think their needs are?" Instead of planning on your own, you need to assess your workforce's needs, consider the type of work people do, and, most importantly, listen to employees.

Aligning with Employee Needs and Employer Priorities

As we detailed in Chapter 5, surveys, focus groups and meaningful conversations with employees are the keys to understanding the range of challenges employees face. For example, an employer in which most employees sit for long stretches at their computers may want to emphasize changes to ergonomics and office design, as well as fitness challenges and walking meetings. A workforce with many "panini generation" employees may prioritize child-care and elder-care EAP counseling, as well as on-site yoga and other stress-reducers. Further, health risk assessments can give you information on which programs might generate the most interest and make the most impact.

Our programs should also be aligned with organizational priorities. For example, part of the success of Johnson & Johnson's pioneering smoking cessation program in the late 1980s was how well this initiative was connected to its company-wide focus on health care[26]. Likewise, UnderArmor's gym and fitness offerings are a natural complement to its culture and the types of products it offers.[27] Leonard Berry describes a well-aligned approach at Chevron[28]:

> *Take Chevron, where 60% to 70% of all jobs are considered safety-sensitive, in that employees put themselves or others at risk. Fitness for duty is a central concern on oil platforms and rigs, in refineries, and during the transport of fuel. To reinforce the mantra that healthy workers are safer workers, Chevron has developed a strong wellness program that includes a comprehensive cardiovascular health component, a 10K-a-day walking activity, fitness centers, a repetitive-stress-injury prevention program, and work/life services.*

Finally, as with any other employee-related program, you want to involve employees in planning. By doing so, you'll more directly address their concerns and be more confident you are spending your limited resources in the most efficient manner.

Publicity and Incentives

Once you craft your wellness program, you need to make sure to publicize the program and promote its use[29]. There are many ways to do this. First, leadership needs to be highly involved with program launch and subsequent company-wide communication. Ideally, they should serve as visible role-models of program use (e.g., once the CFO starts using the fitness center, others will follow...). Without visible leadership buy-in, wellness programs run the risk of being considered "just another HR initiative" with potentially limited credibility. C-level attention provides a powerful social cue.

Second, you should promote your program through many communication channels. Lots of companies launch with a "wellness fair" in which the full range of services are presented, employees can sign up for programs, and outside care professionals come in to conduct HRAs. Beyond a kick-off event, you can gather links to your programming onto a single online platform and then use a diversity of media to bring employees to that site.

Further, you need to bring your communications directly to your employees. Company-wide emails and newsletters may be ignored by busy employees, but face to face conversations in the break room, cafeteria, or at the beginning of weekly department meetings can get your message through. Creative touches, such as putting signs in the elevators to encourage people to take the stairs, delivering fruit baskets to the break room, or setting up a smoothie bar in the lobby, can generate attention.

Next, you need to ensure your programs are accessible and easy-to-use. For example, according to SAS Software's Jack Poll, part of the success of their on-site fitness center is its accessibility[30]:

Our high participation rates are because, when we opened, we thought of all the reasons people wouldn't use the facility and we worked to eliminate every one of them. The center is open before and after work and on weekends, and our staff develops a variety of fresh, engaging programs.

Using similar logic, you'll get more people to enroll in a "10,000 step challenge" if you provide fitness trackers free of charge. People will go to blood pressure screenings and get flu shots if you conduct them in the centrally-located conference room during normal work hours, as opposed to having people wait in a long line in the lobby at the end of the workday. Further, making our programming accessible to remote workers, especially during Covid, requires creativity.

Once launched and accessible, you need to motivate employees to participate in your programming. By offering group activities, such as fitness challenges or outdoor adventures, you can generate enthusiasm and peer support. Gamification techniques, in which participants "level up" as in a video game while earning badges, coupons, or small rewards, are fun ways to encourage participation[31]. Finally, incentives can be effective in encouraging employee uptake. Just make sure that rewards are small, appropriate, and prioritize participation as opposed to competition. Bill Plastine at BASF describes a well-crafted wellness program and how they motivated employees to participate:

We had a fitness tracker step challenge and gave people Amazon gift cards for participating. This was a good community-building exercise, and we even created a little bit of friendly competition between teams.

Assessment and Continuous Improvement

Of course, once programs are up and running, you need to collect feedback to determine which aspects are working well and which need to be improved. To this end, Cambia Health Solutions conducts an annual wellness survey to get feedback on its wellness offerings and makes changes accordingly.

Finally, collecting evaluation data on your program is critically important. Of course, you should track participation and health outcomes. In addition, demonstrating a return on investment for your programs[32], for example, through reductions in health care, disability, and workers' compensation costs, will enable you to expand your programming over time.

A COMPREHENSIVE WHOLE-PERSON APPROACH TO EMPLOYEE WELLNESS

Tony Bridwell, CHRO of Ryan, LLC, describes employee wellness as a central component of their new RyanThrive initiative. His description of this program provides an example of a well-crafted, strategically-aligned, and intelligently implemented wellness program.

At Ryan we had a long list of benefits and programs that we offered, but these were too scattered. Some employees didn't know all we offered, and few saw how they really fit together to support them as whole people. We were spending money on these programs and doing a lot, but weren't having the full impact we could have.

With the RyanThrive wellness initiative we started in 2019, we can now show what we do to help our employees in their careers, financially, with their physical and emotional well-being, and how we create and support our community. By bringing in so much of what we already did, plus new initiatives, into a single aligned approach makes our range of programs easier to understand- they're not just initiatives scattered about. This approach has had much more impact.

We have a consolidated platform that employees can access anytime, anywhere, to proactively manage their own wellbeing.

It all starts with a personal well-being assessment as their introduction to the Thrive platform. They assess along four areas of thriving- career/purpose, physical, financial, and emotional (which includes social and community). All this is confidential, and only seen by the employee, and it helps them assess areas they want to prioritize and the resources and programs available to them. It's all unique and customized to each employee.

We build on the assessment with awareness, resources, support and follow-up. We're constantly looking at continuous improvement, and we aim to expand on our comprehensive view of thriving and well-being as a way to separate ourselves from other employers.

Specifically, in terms of physical health and wellness, we have lots of activities and workplace challenges. A lot of these are points-based and gamified. For example, we had teams versus teams steps challenges and a 150-minutes exercise challenge. Offices and teams around the country compete. We have a range of programs to encourage and support healthy lifestyles, and referral services for specific areas of need.

And here's the payoff. First, we have more employees thriving in more areas of their lives- which is of course the most important thing. Employees can spend their life thriving or struggling in key areas of their lives. We have to ask how we can help all of us get to thriving in all those areas. If you think about, and provide a wide range of support, for the employee to thrive as a whole person, then the value proposition goes off the chart.

Just on health care spending alone- research shows that those who thrive in most areas average $4000 a year, and those struggling average over $12,000. And this doesn't even get to the benefits of engagement and productivity. A thriving, healthier workforce is great for everyone.

And, as a company, we have three overarching measures. First, we assess how well our employees are thriving. Next, we measure our client experience and satisfaction. And, finally, of course, we measure our company value through top and bottom line growth. All three are intrinsically linked- it's hard to excel in one without excelling in all three.

In short, Ryan has integrated physical and mental wellbeing with other Whole-Person Workplace initiatives to create a comprehensive, easily communicated approach that registers with employees. Employee wellness is part of the core of how they manage and measure organizational performance. Wellness is built into, and helps promote, their culture.

THE FINAL WORD

Employees are whole people, including their bodies and minds. Robert Russo of Bristol-Myers Squibb explains it well, "If you only recognize 60% of who [employees] are, you only get 60% of them. You don't get the 100% or everything you can."

When employees are healthy, they feel better about themselves and have the energy they need to rise to the challenges they face at work, home, and life. Whole-Person Workplaces would be wise to develop a wide range of initiatives to support employees' physical and mental health, geared to their specific needs. For some, this means support for exercise; for others, it means counseling services through an EAP. Workplace design is also important. Let's make our wellness programs so motivating that some employees will never take the elevator again!

IDEAS AND ADVICE

» Wellness programs directly support the physical and mental health and well-being of employees. They should play an integral role in building a Whole-Person Workplace.

» Wellness programs have been linked to a wide range of health and psychological benefits for employees, as well as a positive return on investment for employers. The ROI comes from reductions in health care costs and absenteeism, as well as improvements in morale and productivity.

» Many wellness programs begin with an employee health risk assessment (HRA) to better understand employee needs and customize programming. However, despite legal protections, many employees bristle at sharing personal and medical information. You should proceed carefully and implement safeguards for data.

» There are a wide variety of programs included under the broad umbrella of employee wellness. This variety can initially feel daunting but is actually advantageous for those crafting programs. The diversity enables employers to develop flexible, custom-fit approaches for the specific needs of your workforce.

» You can support employee fitness through on-site gyms, as well as subsidizing employee expenditures on memberships and other fitness-related expenses.

» Workplace wellness can also consist of information and support for making more mindful decisions about nutrition, sleep, and mobility. Providing fitness trackers can be particularly useful.

» You can host a variety of activities to encourage fitness at work by bringing in outside experts to work with employees on healthy habits, ask trainers and coaches to guide employees through yoga, meditation, or fitness classes. These programs can be adapted for use by a remote workforce.

» Sedentary office work contributes to a variety of ailments. Better office ergonomics, including standing and walking desks, can a useful solution. Of course, anything we can do to encourage occasional breaks and walking around the building is also helpful.

» Many employees perform physical labor, and their needs for safety and wellness should not be overlooked.

» Workplace design that includes open spaces, natural light, and a connection to nature while encouraging movement is associated with better employee morale and productivity.

» There are a variety of ways you can encourage healthy food choices at work. Cafeterias, meeting food orders, and vending machines can all provide healthier choices. Plus, you can educate your employees so they make better food choices at home and in the food they bring to work.

» Employee Assistance Programs (EAPs) provide a variety of counseling and referral services to help employees with personal problems outside of work. These are becoming increasingly popular and important, especially during the extremely stressful Covid pandemic.

» Engage with employees to learn about their needs- have them help you during the planning process. This will ensure the relevance and impact of your wellness programming. Programs should also be aligned with organizational priorities and values.

» You need to be smart about how you publicize and promote new wellness initiatives. Visible support from top leadership is essential, and you should be creative in developing many ways to market your programs.

» Make sure you craft your programs so they are accessible to employees- provide resources at times and places that are convenient for employees. Then, motivate participation through incentives, gamification, and building a community around wellness programming.

» Evaluate the results of your wellness program using surveys, employee participation data, health outcomes, and ROI through lowered health-related costs.

» RyanThrive is an example of a comprehensive approach to wellness that is well-aligned with strategy and has successfully engaged employees.

CHAPTER 9 – TOWARDS A WHOLE-PERSON WORKPLACE CULTURE

IN THE EARLY DAYS OF Southwest Airlines, they were running out of cash. Back then they had just four planes flying from Dallas to Houston and San Antonio and only several dozen employees. Most companies in their position would have addressed their cash crunch by laying off staff. But not founder/CEO Herb Kelleher. Instead, he sold an airplane[1].

Peter Sammartino dreamed of starting a college to help returning WWII veterans complete their educations, launch into their civilian careers, and educate world citizens, so that just maybe we wouldn't have to suffer through another world war. He built his dream, which is now my employer, Fairleigh Dickinson University[2].

CEO Chieh Huang of Boxed saw the distress of an employee who had taken on a second job to try to save up for his wedding, so he decided to step in and have his company pay for it...

Kristi Bryant walked into Brint Ryan's office to resign...

Dan Price announced a company-wide $70,000 minimum salary and started a freak out...

These stories are known by all employees at these organizations. They illustrate the values held by leadership, demonstrate those values are truly held, and, as a result, help set organizational culture.

Stories are incredibly important to evoke and communicate cultural values. As Julia Beck of the It's Working Project says, "Stories are stickier- we remember stories- data and statistics are great, but people remember the stories- and that can drive change."

Tony Bridwell, CHRO of Ryan, LLC, who was formerly a senior partner at Partners in Leadership, a consultancy that has helped many large companies recharge their cultures, agrees:

> *Stories can change everything. This is the first step in culture building- creating the language of experience. This then leads to action and results. It's all about the stories we tell about how we show up, speak up, and then how these stories interact with processes, policies and procedures. You have to align these so they are consistent over time, impact what people think and feel, influence what they do, and are aligned with our desired outcomes.*

Stories are foundational, but there's also a lot of work behind creating a culture that truly values its employees as whole people[3]. In this chapter, we'll discuss how cultures develop over time and how leaders and policy-makers can change or fortify their company culture. We'll illustrate how leading companies take a comprehensive approach to ensuring that their cultural values are experienced and cherished and lived by their employees and managers. This chapter also pulls together much of the content from prior chapters- after all, so much of what we've covered involves a values-based approach to communicating and enacting our priorities through well-crafted, pro-employee policies.

FOUNDATIONS OF CULTURE

Culture can be defined as a system of shared meaning- the set of shared assumptions, values, and norms that identifies what an organization considers important and how employees and managers should behave[4].

The authentic values of founders and influential leaders make up the heart of organizational culture. Without leadership that embodies Whole-Person Workplace values, this type of culture can never truly take root. Sure, any company can put together a few policies, but after a while, these policies become "policies in name only", and the story around them becomes a cynical tale of employees feeling like the victims of a bait-and-switch- "Sure, they talk all about how they support families, but they wouldn't let me adjust my hours when my daughter was in the hospital."

In well-run organizations, like the ones illustrated at the start of this chapter, the authentic values of leaders are clear for all to see and experience.

ASSESSING CULTURE

The underlying values of your culture may already be consistent with your intentions, or perhaps you feel that your cultural values need to shift. Either way, the first step involves assessing your employees' perceptions of workplace culture.

There are many tools, surveys, and consultancies that can help you do this. But ultimately, most assessments converge on a similar goal- to diagnose the degree to which employees are able to articulate the values of your firm (often referred to of strength of culture), the degree to which employees throughout your company agree on those values, and their importance (often referred to as cohesiveness of culture).

When Tony Bridwell was hired as the CHRO at Ryan, LLC, he was joining a company that largely embodies Whole-Person values. He was brought on to "Strengthen our already strong cultural foundation- tighten and reinvigorate our culture before we embarked on planned growth and expansion."

The first thing he did on the job was interview a wide cross-section of employees, managers, and leadership. He wanted to hear how they described Ryan, its culture, and its approach to accountability. By doing this, Bridwell was able to assess whether employees were aligned around Ryan's desired results and purpose. He learned what beliefs and stories Ryan employees held as important and their desire for improvements. He was encouraged that more than 90% of employees could cite Ryan's values- a solid base of strength and cohesiveness upon which he could build.

This is not too surprising, as Ryan had long tracked the pulse of its employees through the Fortune Great Place to Work Survey. Bridwell told me:

> We got our scores back three weeks ago and we clocked the highest score in company history at 96% employee engagement. That's just crazy ridiculously high. [CEO] Brint [Ryan] thinks this sets us apart. But now our whole focus is the remaining 4%. We are obsessed with the other 4% and understanding what can we do better, what are we missing. This is part of our continual improvement and growth mindset, which, again, is part of our culture.

In Bridwell's case, his assessment revealed an already strong culture that simply required reinforcement and perhaps some minor tweaking.

In cases where there is a disconnect, it becomes important to collect information on what employees believe the culture of your organization should emphasize and compare those values to your current ones. Conducting this exercise can reveal the most important areas to address in order to recalibrate your culture. Doing this sort of analysis can be especially eye-opening for leadership, who may have been unaware of the unintended signals they may have been sending. Recall Alyssa Westring's story of the senior leader she interviewed (from Chapter 5):

> She would always tell her employees to unplug after hours and to take all their vacation time. But they saw her working all the time, emailing 24/7, and assumed they had to as well. Many didn't want to get promoted because they saw her hours! When she finally realized she had unconsciously shifted the culture it was profound realization for her. Choices leaders make affect others in terms of time use and of prioritizing life.

Regardless of her intent, this leader demonstrated her enacted values around time and life. These actions create a strong narrative around company priorities, one that requires a heavy lift to change. In cases like this, it will require a long-term effort to align employee-related policies to your desired cultural values, changing the over-arching story employees experience.

ALIGNING POLICY TO CULTURAL VALUES

Lisa Evans of Conagra Foods discusses the importance of alignment:

> *I've worked in companies that were kicking off new values but their actions didn't support them. Obviously, these efforts didn't really work. What you need to do, like we do here, is make sure your HR and other policies match your values, and that they are integrated into the culture. This takes time, and there's no 'secret sauce.' It depends on lots of people working in line with our priorities- making decisions about 'is this the right thing to do?', looking at the results, and truly showing up as leaders.*

Evans makes it clear that the next critically important aspect of building a culture is translating cultural values into policies and programs that employees experience. After all, stated values aren't your true actual values unless you follow through on them, especially when it might be difficult or inconvenient to do so[5].

So far in this book, we've seen many examples of values being translated into policies and policies that reinforce those values. For example, as discussed in Chapters 6 and 7, Johnstone Supply embeds their values into much of how they operate, including how they hire employees and evaluate performance. According to CHRO Chris Geschickter:

> *We are a family-owned company- the founders started the company because they wanted contractors to get a better customer experience- and we have a very family feel. When I was hired 2 years ago, I didn't have to sell them on the importance of core values and managing towards them. They already knew and promoted this. It's how we hire and keep employees...*

When we do performance reviews, our values are our leading criteria. In fact, the majority of how we do performance evaluation is by reflecting on our core values- and then assessing whether an employee's behavior is aligned with them- in terms of customer service, teamwork, and such. We really drill down to describing behavior aligned with these core values. What does behavior that is an excellent representation of our values look like? What's a good representation? What isn't satisfactory? These behavioral examples are really helpful. To us, performance evaluation is a conversation throughout the year, and a lot of self-evaluations.

I often work with companies that intend to change their culture around such policies as parental leave and flexibility. Many of those I work with have identified these supports as important, but they had not yet been able to translate these values into policies that employees trust enough to use.

I worked with a financial firm that offered generous leave policies but also exhibited a hard-charging "work first" culture. New leadership truly wanted more men to take paternity leave and were frustrated that employees were reluctant to take them at their word that they'd be supported in taking leave. New fathers at this firm had long known that extended leaves had torpedoed careers and reputations. No doubt, they all remembered stories of those who had washed out, or those "heroes" who came back to work they day after their spouse gave birth. They saw who got promoted 8 months later and who did not[6].

Leadership asked me what it would take for men in their organization to feel comfortable taking long paternity leaves. I told them they wouldn't like my answer, because it is not an easy thing to do. It couldn't be changed just by implementing thoughtful policy. Rather, it takes 3-5 years of consistent decision-making, messaging, communication, role-modeling, and follow-through to change the stories around fatherhood and parental leave[7].

It takes a long time for employees to trust that substantive change is real. In this case, they need to see visible role models- male leaders taking leave and continuing to advance in their careers[8]. They require comprehensive communication and support around leave, including manager training, a program for planning for leave (like we discussed in Chapter 3), and consequences for those blocking the new culture.

Only over a long period of time will the stories change, so that employees remember that guy from their department who took all eight weeks and then continued on his trajectory. Or the time when their coworker took his full paternity leave and, because the team planned ahead and created a developmental opportunity for a junior staffer, no one felt overburdened. Culture change takes time and persistence.

CHANGING CULTURE TO REFLECT WHOLE-PERSON VALUES

Beyond a genuine commitment by leadership, there are several critically important ways to change culture over time, or to reinforce an already strong culture. These include human resources policies, workplace metrics, resource allocation, visible symbols, and statements of values.

Culture Change Through Human Resources Policy

Chapters 6 and 7 explicitly make the case for embedding Whole-Person Workplace values into how we hire, orient new employees, evaluate performance, and make decisions about compensation and benefits. Several great examples we've covered include: how Johnstone Supply hires for both skills and culture; how Flexjobs use creative ways to fully integrate new employees during orientation; how Ryan evaluates employee performance; how Uncommon Goods structures its pay system to respect and support all employees; and how Costco provides health insurance and retirement plans to its part-time hourly workforce.

Zappos.com provides an illustrative example[9]. As we covered earlier, Zappos conducts two sets of interviews during the hiring process- one for qualifications and the other for fit with their cultural values (customer service, bringing your whole self to work, teamwork). During the 5-week new employee orientation, all employees undergo customer service training and several days' orientation on culture. After orientation, new employees who feel as if they don't fit are offered a quitting bonus (currently over $3000). At Zappos, employees are evaluated not just on their work but also on whether they are living and spreading company values.

SAS, a leading provider of data analytic software also takes a comprehensive approach. Beyond quality hiring, orientation. and performance evaluation, SAS provides a suite of benefits that are consistent with Whole-Person values[10]. For example, they provide on-site child-care at their North Carolina headquarters, as well as an on-campus gym and fitness center, a wide range of wellness programs, a high-trust approach to workplace flexibility, and an array of educational and developmental opportunities. At both of these leading employers, HR practices are fully aligned with culture, reinforcing it at every step of the employee experience.

Culture Change Through Workplace Metrics

There's an ongoing debate in management circles. One side contends that, "if you can't measure something, you can't manage it.[11]" Others claim that measurement often creates narrow, rigid, and sometimes nonsensical definitions of success[12]. Of course, many metrics are misaligned, leading to ineffective and even unethical behavior (e.g., the widespread fraud at Wells Fargo in 2016 was accelerated by a singular focus on opening new accounts over other measures of performance[13]). Other times, an exclusive focus on quantitative measurables obscures insights you can only learn from talking with employees and hearing their stories. Overall, the truth, as in most things, lies somewhere in the middle.

I'm a believer in well-crafted, adaptable metrics, especially those that are well-aligned with your priorities and that lend themselves to corrective action. It is important to track such things as employee engagement, stress, retention, and use of available benefits- and to break these numbers down by department, division, location, and leader. By doing so, we can find problems and then explore solutions.

For example, if the turnover rate of people of color is considerably higher in some divisions than others, we can further investigate and root out core problems. Likewise, if we track the use of vacation time, we may learn that usage at one location is half the company average, and then intervene with local managers to correct the situation. Tony Bridwell recommends:

> *You need to hold managers accountable. For example, you should measure things like turnover and engagement scores in their groups, and then couple these with incentives. Without measurement, you can't build accountability. And without accountability, then it is just discretional to be a good manager.*

Further, we should also measure progress on particularly important goals or areas in which we know we need to improve. For example, companies that have struggled with gender equity need to track the degree to which they provide equal opportunities to women, satisfaction with mentoring efforts, whether there is evidence of unconscious bias in performance evaluations, and what might be blocking women from progressing in their careers.

Johnstone Supply, once again, provides us a model. From CHRO Chris Geschickter:

> *You have to ask- Are you really addressing their needs or just what you think their needs are? We recently conducted our annual employee engagement survey. We took our results at group level and region by region. We met as an executive team to talk through the results. We came up with three changes, shared these plans with employees to let know what we are doing in*

response to their feedback, and are committed to maintaining transparency and accountability.

By measuring our progress, we better understand what we are doing right (and then can reinforce it) and better know what needs fixing. After all, how else can Bridwell figure out how to reach the other 4%?

Culture Change Through Resource Allocation

Budgets aren't just financial planning documents; they are also tangible reflections of organizational values[14]. For example, a company can profess that it is dedicated to employee development but betray this stated value by cutting the training budget at the first sign of financial difficulty.

On a more positive note, many "essential employers" provided a bonus to employees who continued working during the pandemic and spent considerable sums to enhance worker safety[15]. This was not only done out of business necessity or the desire to retain employees concerned about Covid. In many cases, these were provided as tangible expressions of commitment to employees.

Some companies go so far as to specifically budget money and staff lines for their organizational culture. By earmarking money for culture-building activities and for a "culture officer" or "culture whip" position[16], you embed cultural values into your formal budget process.

As we have seen, firms like Gravity Payments and Uncommon Goods provide livable wages that are higher than their competitors. While there are certainly business reasons to do so- to attract, retain and engage quality employees- both firms expressly state that their salary structures were informed by their Whole-Person Workplace values. Recall the quote from Chapter 7, "Don't tell me where your priorities are. Show me where you spend your money, and I'll tell you what they are."

Culture Change Through Visible Symbols

While visible symbols are not the most important element of culture, they can play a role in reminding employees of sincerely held values. For example, Zappos' relaxed style of teamwork is complemented by their casual dress policy and open workspaces that employees are encouraged to customize and decorate as they see fit. Similarly, Southwest Airline's unofficial motto is "Love"- in part because it encapsulates their culture, in part because they were founded at Dallas' Love Field airport. Their logo is a heart with wings, and their stock ticker symbol is LUV!

Salesforce reinforces their core value of "Ohana," the Hawaiian word for family. This word is a verbal reminder of their core values- "trust, customer success, innovation, giving back, equality, wellness, transparency, and fun[17]." The word, "Ohana" is seemingly everywhere on the company website, at the workplace, and in its public statements. Because Salesforce actually does create a family atmosphere and lives its stated cultural values, everyone seems to buy into the concept, even if it might seem hokey from the outside.

However, employers need to be careful with their use of these gestures. If mottos and symbols come off as insincere or do not match employee experiences, they will be counter-productive. Employees are smart, and they know when they are being patronized or lied to. Better to work on changing your values, policies, and core narratives first before working on symbols.

The best story I ever heard about a disconnect between symbols and culture comes from the book *Rivethead*[18] by Ben Hamper, about his experiences working at a General Motors assembly line in the 1980s. He and his fellow workers were demoralized owing to what they perceived as poor management, a lack of empowerment, and less-than-high-quality work processes. However, in an effort to demonstrate its commitment to quality, management at GM, in a stunningly tone-deaf decision, introduced a costumed mascot, Quality Cat, who visited assembly plants to cheer on employees. You can probably guess how well that went over. One employee:

> *I don't find anything the least bit humorous about having some idiot in a cat's costume roamin' through my place of work. What they are tellin' us is that we are so stunted growth-wise that all we can relate to are characters along the lines of Saturday morning cartoon figures. Bring out Bozo! Hail Huckleberry Hound!*[19]

Predictably, Quality Cat was the recipient of the frustration and ire of this proud but insulted workforce. The mascot was quickly put out of its misery.

Less dramatically, some companies pay little attention to the symbolic messages they send to employees. This often reflects their failure to recognize the importance of culture or situations in which values have drifted from their roots. For example, I remember entering the main lobby of Lucent Technologies (now Alcatel-Lucent, acquired by Nokia) about twenty years ago. Above the registration desk was a huge screen with a minute-by-minute readout of Lucent's stock price. In an otherwise attractive but spare lobby, your eyes couldn't help but be drawn to the image. I met with managers during my visit, and some of them spoke very sincerely about company values.

However, I couldn't shake the notion that the over-riding and unintended message to employees was what they saw at the very beginning and end of every work day. Share price is surely important to stockholders and top management, who I presume came up with the idea for the display. However, it is of less practical importance for most employees. It struck me that a singular visible focus on share price communicated that the stockholder- not quality, innovation, or employees- is the priority.

At the time, Lucent was doing cutting-edge technological research that greatly advanced cellphone and communication technology. They also had a proud history as Bell Labs (AT&T's technology arm before

Ma Bell/AT&T was broken up in the mid-1980s)[20]. It struck me that management could have used every opportunity to remind employees of the significance, purpose, and intrinsic value of their work instead of prioritizing short-term (indeed minute-by-minute) financial performance. Even worse, my visits came at a time when its stock price plummeted (In the first six months of 1999, it fell from $112 to $56 a share)- it may have been demoralizing to see the numbers go down each day.

Contrast this with the lobby at BASF's US headquarters. The lobby highlights recent product innovations and the progress of their sustainability programs- with samples, video screens, and interactive displays. Great for visitors, of course. But also a quick, twice-a-day visual reminder for employees of BASF's values.

Culture Change Through Values Statements

Most companies make a public pronouncement of their values. For some, these statements are sincere reflections of company priorities and what leadership reinforces through culture and policy. For others, it is a cynical exercise to look good (Enron's stated values: "a global corporate citizen that leads through respect, integrity, communication, and excellence"[21]). For many firms, value statements are, well, fine, but don't really move the needle.

Patrick Lencioni makes a persuasive case that official statements of company values are extremely tricky to pull off[22]. He makes crucial distinctions between four different types of values: core, aspirational, permission to play, and accidental.

First, **core values** are what we most often think of when we discuss culture. In order for something to become a core value, it needs to be fully supported, even if doing so incurs costs or limits opportunities. In the prior example, instead of changing nothing and introducing a mascot, GM could have improved their production process or empowered employees to support their stated value of quality.

More specifically for the values espoused in this book, true Whole-Person Workplace values mean prioritizing employee well-being over short-term financial considerations. It means supporting employees who take their full parental leave, even when they are a critical part of an important work project. It means spending money matching charitable donations or providing quality health insurance, instead of solely enriching stockholders. It means, like at Gravity Payments, top management takes a pay cut in order to provide livable wages. In short, there must be an opportunity cost to living core values.

Core values also need to be weaved into many work processes and polices. The prior section on cultural alignment and human resource policies provides some instructive examples. As this book has advocated, Whole-Person values can be promoted in many ways, including: reacting to the Covid pandemic, supporting flexible work arrangements, crafting generous leave polices, assisting new parents, supporting continuing education, promoting volunteerism, providing livable wages, redesigning work to allow more autonomy, supporting the use of paid time off, and developing wellness programs. Without a sufficient investment in at least a critical mass of these programs, Whole-Person values will not become core values.

Relatedly, there's an important distinction between core values and **aspirational values**. It is, of course, laudable, for example, to want to become a more innovative company. However, it would probably be a mistake to declare "innovation" as a current core value before you undertake sufficient efforts to become more innovative. Employees are smart and know the score- their stories of the workplace don't yet reflect an orientation towards innovation. Therefore, even sincere aspirational statements may be rejected if they are presented as current core values. For now, innovation is an aspirational value- it can become a core value over time and with concerted effort.

As an example, some years ago, my university adopted the motto, "The leader in global education," to mixed reviews. While global education goes back to our founder's vision (see the opening to this chapter), we're a mid-sized school without the resources of brand-name globe-spanning universities. However, we do punch above our weight class in terms of international programs, study abroad, and other indicators of a commitment to global education, and we continue to expand these offerings. So, this motto is not without foundation. However, the motto was not initially accepted because it was more aspirational than real. Incidentally, a few years later, new leadership made this very clarification, leading to more accurate messaging and greater employee buy-in.

Many companies are criticized for parroting generic core values. From Lencioni's article:

> *Consider the motherhood-and-apple-pie values that appear in so many companies' values statements- integrity, teamwork, ethics, quality, customer satisfaction, and innovation. In fact, 55% of all Fortune 100 companies claim integrity is a core value, 49% espouse customer satisfaction, and 40% tout teamwork. While these are inarguably good qualities, such terms hardly provide a distinct blueprint for employee behavior. Cookie-cutter values don't set a company apart from competitors; they make it fade into the crowd.*

He labels these commonly-espoused generic statements as **"Permission to Play" values**. This means that, of course, any company worth its salt will have a baseline intolerance for a lack of integrity. But unless you intend to value integrity more than other companies or more than other values, integrity is a fine sentiment- but not a "core value." Promoting permission to play values as core values runs the risk of generating apathy rather than motivation. (As counter-examples, Zappos and Johnstone Supply do follow-through on customer service as a legitimate core value.)

Finally, **accidental values** become adopted over time if leadership doesn't pay sufficient attention to building and reinforcing its culture. Often, this represents an unthinking drift away from formerly core values. After all, if "excellence in customer service" isn't reinforced through training, performance evaluation, bonuses, and managerial role-modeling, why should employees devote extra effort towards that goal? Similarly, if, despite half-hearted attempts to improve parental leave policies, taking a long leave is still considered career suicide, why would anyone buy in? Accidental values are the counter-productive residue of the failure to truly uphold stated values.

Regardless of the values you espouse, the most important lesson is that what truly matters are your **enacted values**. For example, while New Moon Natural Foods has a values statement which they take very seriously, founder and president Billy Griffin believes that actions speak louder than words. He abides by the classic lyric from legendary reggae musician Peter Tosh, "Live clean; let your works be seen[23]". Griffin continues, "We actively promote our values, but we don't boast about them. Instead it's what we do every day- maintaining an authentic, giving culture. Employees and customers will tell your story for you if you continue to do the right things."

A COMPREHENSIVE APPROACH TO BUILDING A WHOLE-PERSON CULTURE

Many of the examples I've presented in this book may seem skewed towards white-collar professionals and their employers. I'd like to take the opportunity to highlight a comprehensive example of a Whole-Person workplace culture for manufacturing employees, using the example of BASF. Bill Plastine explains:

> In manufacturing, the price of entry is assuring the safety and well-being of employees. Our employees work with chemicals and in facilities that require lots of attention to safety requirements. Employees are smart, and when we interview them, they want to know how long the site has been incident-free, how long has it been since a reportable accident? What helps us is how we treat

employees- we talk about how we care about people and their safety, that we want them to return home healthy.

Beyond that, we offer a diversified approach to total compensation, ranging from parental leave, pet insurance, and a whole host of over 100 benefits geared to the stressors of full-time physically demanding work [the BASF website cleverly displays its programs using a 'periodic table of benefits[24]*].*

Our manufacturing employees make great use of our tuition reimbursement programs- which can be used for colleges, technical schools, online courses, certificate programs, and community colleges- Night programs in the skilled trades. Because we have lots of different types of employees, we try to extend a wide range across the whole organization and then people can choose what works for them. At one facility, we have a partnership with a local community college- they can go there for free and take courses in specialized areas that are relevant to the work at our site. For us, skill-building is very important.

Employee recognition is really important at the local level. Some plants have as few as 70 employees. We do a good job in recognizing milestones, like 20 years of service, recognizing their commitment- and coming from management that means a lot.

We also offer general wellness benefits. During the height of Covid, when most gyms were closed, we reimbursed employees for buying fitness equipment. We provided virtual nutrition counseling. We also had a fitness tracker step challenge, and gave people Amazon gift cards for participating. This was also a good community-building exercise.

Clearly, this thoughtful and comprehensive approach to building a culture around safety, development, and recognition of employees is relevant for any employer. The mix of what you offer reflects your desired and actual cultural values. Choose generously and with care.

———

THE FINAL WORD

Building a culture that helps you attract, retain, and engage quality employees will help your company achieve long-term, sustainable success in a wide variety of strategic and competitive contexts. But great cultures don't build themselves. Rather, they are based on the genuine values of leadership and communicated to employees primarily through a wide variety of employee-related policies and decisions that affect their daily work lives.

Tony Bridwell counsels, "We can accelerate cultural change by pulling certain cultural levers. But you have to know which ones to pull." To promote Whole-Person values, you need to assess and reorient your HR policies, resource allocation, measurements, and messaging. Even in the best companies, if you don't consistently put in the required work, you'll never be able to engage the remaining 4%.

IDEAS AND ADVICE

» Culture involves the shared values in a company, as reflected in the stories employees tell about their work lives and in the accumulation of policies and decisions that affect them.

» Assessing employee perceptions of culture through surveys and conversations is the starting point to understand current culture and what may need to be done to either reinforce or reorient your culture.

» The key to building culture is aligning leadership actions, decision-making, and human resources policies to reflect core values. Achieving significant culture change can take up to 3-5 years of consistent action.

» Measurement and budgeting are fundamental to running any business. Smart use of workplace metrics and resource allocation can reinforce cultural values.

» Visible symbols are important for highlighting truly held core values. However, if core values are not truly supported, symbolic gestures will foster cynicism.

» Many companies codify their cultures into statements of values. However, care must be taken to ensure that you are living out core values. Purely aspirational statements and generic platitudes are far less impactful and may be counter-productive.

CHAPTER 10 – TAKING ACTION IN YOUR SPHERE OF INFLUENCE: LESSONS FOR LEADERS, SUPERVISORS, HR PROFESSIONALS, SMALL-BUSINESS OWNERS, INDIVIDUAL CONTRIBUTORS, AND JOB-SEEKERS

A s the reality of Covid struck Bristol-Myers Squibb in early 2020, HR Executive Bob Russo remembers conversations he had with leadership on how they would adapt:

> *We needed to explore all ideas, and instead of asking how or why we might do something, we need to instead, ask 'why not?' Let's explore all ideas. We were already in a place where we were changing work dynamics. I mean, are we going to buy laptops for 35,000 employees? Why? Why not? We have to take all constraints off our thinking. In our ideation, we have to ask what is possible? We can't do everything, but we need to ask that question.*

I hope we never find ourselves in such a crisis again. However, Russo makes an important point. The key to progress is taking constraints off our thinking, so we can consider the widest array of ways to support our employees and enable them to perform.

I wrote *The Whole-Person Workplace* with a variety of readers in mind—top leadership, supervisory management, human resources professionals, small business owners, individual contributors, and job-seekers. It is my fervent hope that the book has helped spark many ideas of how you can make changes to, or better navigate, your organization.

In this final chapter, I highlight some of the book's most important lessons to help you embed Whole-Person values into your sphere of influence. I hope you "ask 'why not?'" as you, no doubt, develop your own creative solutions to the specific challenges you and your employees face.

ACTION STEPS FOR ORGANIZATIONAL LEADERS

As organizational leaders, you set the course for organizational culture through your words and especially your actions. Employees, HR departments, and individual managers may advocate for change, but when leadership gets involved, meaningful change can happen- and happen fast.

There were many at Ryan, LLC, including Delta Emerson, who had advocated for changes to the workplace. There were many employees like Kristi Bryant, for whom the "long hours culture" made them consider leaving. However, when CEO G. Brint Ryan got on board, their transformation to a flexible workplace began in earnest[1]. His leadership lent the effort instant credibility and access to the resources it needed to implement its workplace flexibility program.

Addressing Whole-Person Concerns by Listening to Diverse Perspectives

Relatedly, while many CEOs endeavor to hear from a wide variety of employees, it is true that most work closely with a finite set of leaders and managers. The composition of your leadership inner circle is incredibly important. If this group lacks diversity, the quality of leadership decisions diminishes[2]. Diverse leadership teams, in terms of demographics, professional background, and personality/working style, help you appreciate a wider set of perspectives and alternatives[3].

Diversity at the top is particularly important for Whole-Person Workplaces. If leadership is composed primarily of older white men whose life experiences have not led them to grapple with issues relating to workplace discrimination, gender and racial equity, or work-family pressures, it is likely their conversations and decisions may not fully reflect today's challenges. Even well-intentioned executives have blind spots. Ensuring that women and people of color have integral roles in top-level decision making makes it much more likely you'll consider a full range of perspectives before taking action. Your company must be a place where all employees are valued and can bring their whole selves to work. This requires prioritizing diversity to ensure a well-rounded perspective.

This also underscores the importance of measuring the results of employee-related programs and taking corrective actions when necessary. If working mothers and fathers who visibly use work-family benefits face negative career consequences and, therefore, cannot rise to leadership positions, you won't get their perspective. And, of course, this tendency is even more insidiously true if conscious or unconscious discrimination against minorities is allowed to occur unchecked (more on this issue in the Afterword).

Beyond demographic and experiential diversity, your top management team needs to include those who represent employee interests. Labor unions and employee councils should have representation[4]. As we'll discuss in just a few pages, valuing human resources professionals as strategic partners ensures that employee concerns become part of every conversation.

In recognition of HR's importance for strategy formation and implementation, most large companies now have a Chief Human Resources Officer, on par with other C-level executives[5] (the old model of a VP of HR reporting to a CFO or COO is thankfully on the wane). An empowered CHRO informs strategic decision-making and sends a clear signal of the centrality of Whole-Person Workplace perspectives.

Balancing Short-Term and Long-Term Priorities

One of the major barriers to implementing Whole-Person Workplace policies is the tug-of-war many leaders face between short-term financial imperatives and long-term investments. It is true that most pro-employee programs involve up-front costs. After all, the P in PTO stands for "paid." However, the return on investment for these programs are real- even if they show up in the longer-term. Recall Josh Bersin's accounting of the costs of turnover from the Introduction, which include the cost of hiring and onboarding a new person, lost productivity and engagement, customer service errors, training costs, and negative cultural impact[6].

SAS software provides an illustrative example. With the full support of co-founder and CEO Jim Goodnight, SAS has built a world-class Whole-Person Workplace. As a privately-held firm, SAS can prioritize the long-term over the often overly-short-term imperatives that publicly-traded companies face[7]. CHRO Jenn Mann explains:

> *We have a very comprehensive benefits package: sick pay, healthcare, vacation and pension plans... but where SAS has really gotten a lot of recognition are the what I would consider the non-traditional benefits, things like an on-site childcare facility, spa services- so pedicures and manicures, three full-service cafes. We have on-site car detailing, we have dry cleaning services, a recreation and fitness facility that's just incredible, we have summer camps for school-aged children. All of these benefits are here to help make life a little easier for our employees to reduce stress and distractions so that they can focus on being innovative in their work[8].*

As SAS explains, with turnover a quarter of the industry average, 45 well-qualified applicants for every open position[9], and an average employee tenure of 12.4 years[10] (as opposed to the industry average of 4.2), their compensation, benefits, and training programs more than pay for themselves. Plus, longer-tenured, more engaged employees do better work and provide better customer service. This all adds up to a highly successful company and a workplace that fully values its employees as whole people.

SAS's example can seem daunting. Don't despair; every company has to start somewhere, and there are lots of ideas in this book on ways to begin. Further, if you need some structure to start you on your journey, you may want to consider following external guidelines and award criteria. For example, Uncommon Goods became a B-corporation, and then used those guidelines for continuous improvement in a range of areas[11]. Ryan began participating in Fortune's Best Places to Work survey in 2004. Delta Emerson confesses, "We participated in the Fortune Great Place to Work survey, which we miserably lost for many years. But we used all that data to figure out what we needed to do to get where we are today.[12]"

Leadership Messaging and Role-Modeling

Finally, in this book, I have highlighted several CEOs who both provide consistent messaging about and role-model their Whole-Person values, including Dave Bolotsky of Uncommon Goods, Dan Price of Gravity Payments, and Chieh Huang of Boxed. I'd like to share one more story. At the 2014 White House Summit on Working Families, EY's then-CEO Mark Weinberger told an anecdote that, to me, represents corporate leadership that recognized the importance of work-family balance and Whole-Person Workplace values[13].

In his address, Weinberger described how, before accepting the CEO position, he discussed the opportunity with his wife and four children. They agreed that he could take the job only if he remained a highly-involved dad. Shortly after becoming CEO, he was in China giving his first big speech to EY partners. He was nervous about the speech and wanted it to be memorable. There was to be a big dinner reception afterwards. Weinberger gave his speech but ended it with an apology- he would have to skip the reception to get right on a plane back home, so he could take his daughter to her driver's test. He had promised her he'd be there and needed to keep his commitment to his family. «Everyone remembered that. No one remembered my speech.»

Although he was just trying to be a good dad, it turned out that his flight back to his daughter's driving test became a story repeated many times throughout EY. The lesson, I think, is that if the CEO acts on his family-related and whole-person priorities, then other employees can, too.

ACTION STEPS FOR SUPERVISORY MANAGERS

The importance of supervisory management to building a Whole-Person Workplace cannot be overstated. You are the front line of organizational culture and the most important contact point for how your employees experience the workplace. Stephanie Smith of DePaul University describes this dynamic well:

> When done right, alternate work arrangements, flextime, remote work- they can all be offered, but it's the culture and supervisor support that is most critical. Having policy on books without the clear support of front-line supervisors means that these programs may not be effective in retaining and engaging productive employees.

Learning About Your Employees' Needs

While leaders focus on big picture issues, supervisors have the opportunity and responsibility to get to know their employees on an individual level. Of course, any good supervisor assesses their team's personalities and working styles to better customize how they motivate employees. However, it is also critical to understand employees' life priorities and challenges. Empathizing with employees builds trusting relationships and opens lines of communication. Importantly, these relationships enable you to work with employees on customized and informal solutions to their issues. As Mika Cross advises, "extend trust first, and then accountability along the way."

For example, you may learn that one of your employees is struggling to manage her aging parent's declining health. You can now approach that employee and co-develop ways she can be supported- extending trust first. Maybe she needs an advance on her accumulated PTO (you could probably get this approved for her if you pulled the right levers). Maybe she needs ad-hoc flexibility to occasionally leave work early while taking work home to finish at night. That's something the two of you can informally arrange. Perhaps she was unaware of available counseling offered by your EAP, and you can put her in touch with those resources. But none of these solutions can occur without listening to your employees, empathizing with their concerns, and providing support.

Embracing Informal Arrangements

In addition, formal policies cannot cover every eventuality. Sometimes, informal arrangements allow employees the space they need to rise to their challenges with minimal disruptions to work. If your workplace culture is supportive of managerial autonomy and employee flexibility, ad-hoc arrangements are relatively easy to implement.

However, if you work in a less supportive culture, informal arrangements become both more important (because there are likely fewer policies for employees) and somewhat trickier to pull off[14]. Discretion and mutual trust become paramount. That said, informal arrangements can often be the most effective tool in your managerial toolbox[15]. Consider this story[16]:

> I work at a global company in which long hours are expected for those trying to move up and get ahead- and I've always been a workhorse. As my daughter started growing up, I felt I was missing too much that I'd never be able to get back. So, I nervously approached my boss about making a few changes. He was surprisingly open to my idea of 'daddy-daughter Wednesdays'

in which I could be home with my daughter and would come in to the office at 1pm... A few years later, my career has kept on keeping on- plus I feel so much more connected with my daughter, and she with me. Sometimes our own anxiety keeps us from asking for what we need- I'm really glad I did.

Understand and Articulate HR and Company Policies

Relatedly, you should become well-versed on the policies and benefits your employer offers. Many employees are unaware of their full range of benefits. Assuming you've built a trusting relationship, they are far more likely to come to you with questions instead of calling HR. One way to increase your knowledge of people-related policy is to build relationships with the HR department, so they can walk you through program offerings. Another good technique is to frequently invite HR representatives to your weekly meetings, so they can share materials and answer questions directly. As someone who works with HR professionals, I can assure you they'd jump at the chance to promote policies directly to employees.

When you are fully informed and able to explain available benefits, your team should feel more comfortable using these programs. For example, in Chapter 3 we discussed that a lack of information is often a barrier to employees understanding the terms of parental leave and the available supports around these programs. Your employee may be having their first child, so of course, she doesn't know what to expect. This could be the fifth time you've had an employee use parental leave, so you can probably handle most questions. The HR department has likely worked with dozens or hundreds and can guide employees through the nitty-gritty details. Supervisors play such an important role in demystifying HR policies for their teams.

Role-Model Whole-Person Values

Finally, perhaps the most important way you can promote Whole-Person Workplace values is to embody them through your actions. Like it or not, you are a role model for your team, and what you do is very much on display. Even if you're straight, consider attending a LGBTQ ERG meeting to become better informed, while sending a signal of support for all your employees. On the flip side, if you are sending emails at midnight, that isn't the only message you send. Intentionally or not, you are also communicating what "the boss" expects in terms of 24/7 availability. This leader understands[17]:

> *I always made sure to discuss my family at work, and people saw that I adjusted my schedule without apology. After a while, more than a few people who worked for me or with me said that, as a manager, I set a good example about family time. They told me it made them feel more comfortable and shaped how they approached work and life.*

Embody Family-Supportive Supervisory Behaviors

Finally, a team of prominent work-family researchers, led by Leslie Hammer and Ellen Kossek, developed a survey tool to measure Family-Supportive Supervisory Behaviors[18] (FSSB). These behaviors fall into four categories: emotional support, instrumental support, role-modeling, and creative work-family management. The items are:

Emotional Support

1. My supervisor is willing to listen to my problems in juggling work and nonwork life.
2. My supervisor takes the time to learn about my personal needs.
3. My supervisor makes me feel comfortable talking to him or her about my conflicts between work and nonwork.
4. My supervisor and I can talk effectively to solve conflicts between work and nonwork issues.

Instrumental Support

5. I can depend on my supervisor to help me support with scheduling conflicts if I need it.

6. I can rely on my supervisor to make sure my work responsibilities are handled when I have unanticipated nonwork demands.

7. My supervisor works effectively with workers to creatively solve conflicts between work and nonwork.

Role Modeling

8. My supervisor is a good role model for work and nonwork balance.

9. My supervisor demonstrates effective behaviors in how to juggle work and nonwork balance.

10. My supervisor demonstrates how a person can jointly be successful on and off the job.

Creative Work-Family Management

11. My supervisor thinks about how the work in my department can be organized to jointly benefit employees and the company.

12. My supervisor asks for suggestions to make it easier for employees to balance work and nonwork demands.

13. My supervisor is creative in reallocating job duties to help my department work better as a team.

14. My supervisor is able to manage the department as a whole team to enable everyone's needs to be met.

This set of behaviors is extremely well-aligned with a Whole-Person Workplace approach and has been linked to a host of benefits for employees and employers[19]. I suggest you use these descriptors to periodically assess whether you are helping your employees with their work-life challenges. If most of your employees can say yes to most of these questions, you are on the right track. If they can't, now you better understand which aspects of your intended Whole-Person approach you need to improve upon.

ACTION STEPS FOR HUMAN RESOURCES PROFESSIONALS

As the specialist department dedicated to employee-related policy, HR plays a central role in creating and maintaining Whole-Person Workplaces. HR thought leader Dave Ulrich codified four important roles for modern HR professionals[20]: administrative expert, employee advocate, change agent, and strategic partner. Each of these roles is important for embedding values throughout your firm.

Exhibit Administrative Expertise

First, as administrative experts, HR professionals are the ones who know the most about recruitment, selection, onboarding, employee development, performance evaluation, compensation, benefits, employee relations, and employment law. You know enough about health insurance, retirement plans, EAPs, and wellness programs to select and monitor your vendors and partners. As we discussed in Chapters 6 and 7, your task as an administrative expert is twofold.

First, you must create high-quality, value-added HR policies and practices. This means designing employee selection processes that distinguish between quality candidates that fit your firm and those that do not. And creating orientation programs that help new employees understand their job and the culture while building positive relationships. And crafting performance evaluation programs that foster communication, development, and flexibility. And writing sexual harassment policies that abide by the law.

Your administrative expertise also means that you must attend to and communicate the details of policy. The procedural elements are so important. As Amy Beacom of CPLL reminded us in Chapter 3:

> It doesn't matter what kind of leave policy you have if you if your procedural elements are screwed up. You need to have a clear policy that is well communicated to employees. Your staff needs to be able to answer questions and help them navigate- 'what about

my insurance?'- you need to have the answer for that. Do you have eligibility forms to fill out? Are they accessible, do managers know about them? The procedural pieces can derail an entire experience. Any company needs to start there.

Second, you need to design HR programs that embed Whole-Person Workplace values into all you do. Employee selection shouldn't just evaluate qualifications- it should also assess whether candidates reflect and can help grow your culture. Orientation programs should clarify the values and expectations at your firm. Performance evaluations should enable flexibility. Sexual harassment policies should ensure swift due process and foster an environment in which all employees feel safe. In short, being an effective administrative expert also means using your expertise to promote Whole-Person Workplace values.

Advocate for Employees

HR's second role is that of employee advocate. In many ways, you are the connective tissue between employees and management. To fulfill this role, you need to do a good job understanding the needs and concerns of your workforce, ensuring these concerns are reflected in managerial decision-making.

We discussed the importance of listening to employees in Chapter 5 and presented several ways to do so. You can gain valuable information through employee surveys, focus groups, and exit interviews, as well as participating in efforts such as the Great Place to Work survey. These formal means of collecting employee perceptions should be supplemented with personal contact with a wide cross-section of employees. As an HR executive at a national pharmacy chain told me, "You have to really listen. Surveys are great, but not enough. Leaders and HR need to engage widely, and managers need to listen and then speak up for their teams."

The next step is harder- ensuring that employee feedback and concerns are put in front of leadership in a way that influences decision-making.

One way to do so is to balance employee stories with hard data. HR needs to be facile in developing and communicating employee-related metrics that can be tied to financial results. It makes sense that the costs of turnover are steep. However, a rigorous calculation of the return on investment of your new initiative to reduce turnover is more persuasive.

Lead Workplace Change

The third role is that of change agent. In this role, HR acts as internal consultants who help leaders uncover areas for improvement, while managing the human side of organizational change. Too often, leaders implement change without taking the time to understand and address employee concerns, leading to unforeseen problems[21]. For instance, many corporate mergers have failed owing to a lack of attention paid to cultural issues[22]. This is one area in which HR's insight into the needs and concerns of your workforce become critical. You can help ensure that planned change takes employee concerns into account, making things better for everyone. Often, HR needs to supplement organizational changes with training, orientation, and short-term bonuses in order to help employees and managers feel comfortable with and motivated by news ways of working.

Strategic Partnership

Ulrich's final HR role is that of a strategic partner. This means HR fully understands company strategy, is well-versed in finance and accounting, and adds value to upper-level decision-making. Chris Geschickter, CHRO of Johnstone Supply, describes this role:

> HR really needs to understand their business and be seen as business partner. You need to prove yourself and get buy-in to become a valued part of the executive team. If you understand the business, then they have credibility in you. If they ask for your insight, you can't just have a generic reply. Your idea really

has to fit the business- or else they won't ask you again. And, yes, your role is to be an advocate for employees, but you have to understand the business side too.

By becoming a credible business partner, you can ensure that employee concerns are included in strategic plans. A strong HR strategic partner can inject an important perspective into planning. For example, "before we decide to acquire that rival firm, do we understand what it may take to reconcile our different cultures and compensation strategies?" or "If we want to expand by 30 locations next year, what will we need to do to staff up successfully?" Better yet, you can provide that staffing plan.

Perhaps most importantly, you can persuade top decision-makers that employee-related concerns are the key to successful strategic implementation. HR can and should make the case that becoming a Whole-Person Workplace sets a firm on a course for long-term sustainable success, no matter how its strategic imperatives may change. This book has hopefully provided evidence that Whole-Person Workplaces are more resilient in the face of crises, more flexible and adaptable to changing circumstances, and impart sustainable advantages in recruitment, retention, and engagement.

Success in All Four Roles

The HR team at Ryan, LLC, exhibited success in all four roles of HR during Ryan's transformation to the flexible results-only-work environment it is today[23]. As employee advocates, they surveyed and listened to employees about what was preventing them from thriving. They enrolled their CEO and top management in understanding the need for workplace flexibility and partnered with them on designing and implementing their strategy. In close collaboration with top leaders, a wide cross-section of managers, and many employees, the HR team led a multi-year change effort. Finally, they brought their administrative expertise to bear as they developed the performance metrics, team orientations, and wellness programs that ensured their change efforts became part of the company's new culture.

Finally, for the foreseeable future, many employees will remain under considerable stress. Covid may be with us for some time. The need for employers to support employees' physical and psychological well-being, I believe, will only increase. HR needs to redouble efforts in this area.

ACTION STEPS FOR SMALL BUSINESS OWNERS

While small businesses may not have the resources or the capacity to enact the same types of policies that larger employers can, they also have some advantages when it comes to developing Whole-Person Workplaces.

First, like organizational leaders, small business owners have a unique opportunity to set the terms of organizational culture through actions, decisions, and resource allocation. As you are visible to all employees, you are the most important role model. Further, when the leader puts their time, attention, and credibility towards a priority, others quickly follow suit.

Next, like supervisors, small business owners have the opportunity to understand each of your employees as individuals. This knowledge enables you to create customized approaches to help them in their particular circumstances. You can also act more quickly and develop informal ways to support employees. With smaller workplaces, genuine commitment to values can rapidly build, change, or maintain your culture. In contrast, change takes much longer in larger companies.

Billy Griffin of New Moon Natural Foods provides an inspiring perspective on what a small business owner can do to embrace Whole-Person values, as well as the rewards for doing so:

> *Small business owners have an advantage because you can make and change the rules- you don't have to get permission from a corporate office. I would encourage other small business owners who want a Whole-Person workplace to think creatively, and*

then just act on it. Be open to customizing things. Your options are as varied as your employees. If it's a kindness you as a person would give to someone else, your business can do this, too.

And it doesn't have to be a grand gesture. Little kindnesses are important. Even sincere gestures like remembering employees' kids' names, and asking them about how they're feeling if they were sick last week. Little things like that mean a lot. As a small business owner, you can decide- I'm going to listen to you as a person like I would a friend, and be empathetic and allow, welcome and encourage this human connection into the workplace. By doing that, you wind up infusing your culture with those values and connections. You can decide to be a 'good guy', and decide that if you can help you will.

Then, and this is the best part, you can create an institution around that. You can model it and train it with your management staff. And there's no other owner or company or organization that can do it like you. There's no other that will do it your way in your industry, area, group of people, with your set of values. There's an art to building these human connections.

If you have this empathy and humanity in yourself, then do it. You don't need permission to be kind. People want to be with good people, and want to show up for them, work with them, be around them, spend time with them. It's also you, and your creativity and your heart. There's only one of those. Don't be afraid to bring your heart into your business. Trust that the ripple effect will be greater than you know.

It's also enormously gratifying to be able to give a little more and make a difference in others' lives. It's personally very rewarding, and it helps me sleep well at night.

ACTION STEPS FOR INDIVIDUAL CONTRIBUTORS

While this book has most directly addressed leaders, managers, and HR professionals, everyone has a role to play in building and perpetuating Whole-Person values. Even if you are not in charge, you can have a profound positive influence on those around you.

Support Your Coworkers

The first and most foundational thing you can do is to get to know your colleagues as people and see what you can do to support them. You can be the employee who goes out of his way to befriend your newly hired coworker- taking her to lunch or introducing her around. These small gestures, especially when someone may be nervous in a new environment, can make all the difference. Remember that "having a best friend at work" is perhaps the single best indicator of long-term satisfaction and engagement[24].

After all, if you and your colleagues are going to spend 40-50 hours a week at the workplace, it would be a missed opportunity to fail to create friendships. For instance, celebrating employee birthdays with cake in the break room is fun! But if no one keeps track of birthdays, collects the money, or buys the cake, there's no party. Workplaces can host baby showers, happy hours, teambuilding lunches, and company picnics. Managers don't always step up to enliven the social side of work. Perhaps you can.

In addition, when managers offer an accommodation to a coworker, it may be human nature to become resentful. Even worse, you- the young, healthy, single guy without kids- may find yourself staying late to pick up the slack. Sure, you can consider yourself the victim of this story[25]. Instead, you can rewrite the script and see yourself as stepping up to support your colleague and work team. After all, caring for a special-needs child with significant health problems as a single parent can't be easy. You don't want to be a doormat, and you deserve to have your manager also attend to your needs, but consider how much you help your colleagues by cheerfully supporting them during their time of need. I'm sure at some point, you'll need others to pitch in for you. Why not contribute to an environment that makes mutual support more likely?

Join Workplace Initiatives

There are also more formal ways you can contribute to building or sustaining a Whole-Person Workplace. Many companies need employees to join employee resource groups, short-term project teams, or long-term committees focused on building a better workplace. By participating in these efforts, you also help yourself- by building your internal network, developing teaming and communication skills, and, of course, improving your workplace.

Role-Model Whole-Person Values

Finally, especially if have job security and a good reputation, we need employees to step up as role-models. Be the first man in your department to take extended parental leave, giving others more confidence they can do it too. And, while you're at it, redouble your efforts to work with your manager and team to ensure your leave works for everyone, reducing the resistance other might face in the future. Be the employee who respectfully gives her boss feedback that her 11pm emails are causing stress for the team. Be the team leader who unapologetically leaves early[26]:

> I coach most of my kids' teams. With my long commute, I have to leave work by about three to get there in time. I plan ahead at work accordingly, and check in with my coworkers. But then I go- I don't flaunt it, but I don't ask for permission, either. My coworkers know I make up the work time either at night or over the weekend. Sometimes, I even trade off some tasks with my friend at work so we can cover for each other if any last minute things come up.

Change doesn't happen unless someone steps up. Maybe the change can come from you.

ACTION STEPS FOR JOB-SEEKERS

In the long-run, you'll have a better and more fulfilling career (and life!) if you take a multifaceted view of what you want in a potential employer and prioritize Whole-Person Workplaces. Of course, pay and benefits are foundational. However, a sole focus on these might mean joining a company that doesn't sufficiently value you as whole person. I'd also be sure to consider whether potential employers offer a wide array of benefits, including work-family supports and wellness programs. Further, support for things like volunteerism, adequate vacation, and a proactive approach to workplace flexibility should be part of your calculus.

Do your research to uncover potential employers with reputations for supporting their employees' life priorities. The Fortune 100, Glassdoor, the Fatherly 50 Best Companies for Working Fathers, and Working Mother Magazine's Best Employer lists can all be valuable resources. Use people in your network to find out more about their companies and get information about aspects of their workplace that you might not have considered before.

When you interview for a job, remember that the best long-term opportunities represent a good fit between your values and the company's culture[27]. If working for a Whole-Person Workplace is important for you, you can ask questions to find out more. For example, I'd recommend some of the following questions to ask at the end of your interviews:

» During the height of Covid and work-from-home, how did your company go out of its way to support employees who may have had a hard time with work-life balance or anxiety?

» Can you tell me about a time when the company stepped up for an employee who was facing a difficult situation in their personal life?

» How does your company keep itself appraised of employee concerns? And how do you respond when you learn that a segment of your workforce is voicing a problem?

» What are some of the most important cultural values at this firm, and how does leadership enact these values to make them real for employees?

» How diverse is your leadership team?

» Can you tell me about someone who, at one point in their career with you, had to alter their work because of life demands, and is now in a position of leadership?

» How do you encourage employees to take all their vacation days, as well as their available parental or family leave?

When you first join a company, you get more of an opportunity to assess its true values. In your first few weeks, you should make friends at work and ask them about their perspectives. Make a special point to network with managers, as well as those in higher positions and in other departments. Also, pay attention to the difference between stated policies and the policies employees use. For example, if your employers offer flextime, but no one ever uses it, you may have a "policy in name only" without the culture to support it.

In the long run, you will do better if you work for a company that matches your values. Maybe you need to stay in a sub-optimal situation for a while, but you should manage your career so you eventually get to employers who properly value their employees.

THE FINAL WORD

No matter your sphere of influence, there are many ways you can help build and sustain a workplace culture that values all employees as whole people. I hope the ideas in this chapter can help you consider creative ways to contribute. It all starts by asking, "why not?" This question can lead you to embrace solutions large and small, expected and unconventional. Who knows, you may even need to buy 35,000 laptops.

Thank you so much for reading, *The Whole-Person Workplace*. I want to end this book by returning to the quote that inspired its title:

We have to realize we get the whole person through the door. We get their backs and their hands and their minds and their hearts, and they're all at different stages in their lives, and we have to make sure we're doing the very best we can to keep them long-term. Because if we do that, they're going to help us succeed.

- Delta Emerson

AFTERWORD – THE IMPORTANCE OF DIVERSITY, EQUITY, AND INCLUSION

JUST AS THE COVID PANDEMIC altered the content of this book, so has the increased (and long overdue) attention to social and racial justice, gender equity, and diversity and inclusion in the workplace[1].

Of course, you cannot have a Whole-Person Workforce if any of your employees do not feel comfortable bringing their whole selves to work. This does not just mean acknowledging their personalities and life challenges, but also essential parts of their identities.

One of the lessons of recent years is that even well-meaning, non-prejudiced individuals can have blind spots about race, gender, sexuality, and other issues that can lead to unconscious bias. Of course, implicit bias training and orientation are important. In addition, we should be more aware that bias is sometimes embedded into processes and structures, so that even fair decision-makers operate in a context that can lead to uneven results.

To combat this, you first need to examine decision-making in your organization for patterns of results over time. If women plateau at a certain level in your company and tend not to progress further, you need to examine why. Perhaps there is overt sexism at your workplace. More commonly, however, unconscious bias (as discussed in Chapter 4) or flaws in work design (Chapter 6) are to blame. In larger organizations, we can collect data broken down by location, department, supervisors, and local leadership. All workplaces need to listen and be alert to systematic problems. If we uncover an issue, we need to address it head on.

A proactive way to address concerns is to bring together a diverse team of employees to participate in systemic solutions- not one-off task forces, but permanent sounding boards. As Dan Domenech, CHRO of Hewlett Packard Enterprises Financial Services states:

The recent unrest on racism and inclusion has led lots of organizations to self-examine. What can we do to make people comfortable bringing their whole selves to work? What policies and programs do we need to help address social injustice? One part of it is providing a forum for people to talk about their experiences and the times they faced micro-aggressions or unconscious bias.

One good way to do this is through Employee Resource Groups, but with a twist. The ERG should not only consist of individuals directly affected by the issue or category- it should also contain a cross-section of leadership and representatives from HR.

For example, an ERG focused on issues of sexuality and gender identity should also include straight allies and members of leadership. ERGs focused on racial justice need to include some white people, including those in decision-making power, so they can better understand issues they might not have previously confronted in their lives and careers. By including leadership and HR representatives, issues brought up in ERGs can more quickly be turned into action.

We also need to examine possible disparities in how a wide range of seemingly neutral policies play out for employees. Over time, for example, small differences in initial pay or salary negotiations build up to significant disadvantages for women and minorities- and these should be rectified.

Many companies recently transitioned to remote work in the wake of the Covid pandemic. However, it is probable that some segments of your workforce were better able to succeed working from home than others[2]. Some work from fully-resourced home offices, with quality Wi-Fi and a family member able to act as a buffer for child-care and online school responsibilities. Others work from an out-of-date laptop on a kitchen table in a crowded apartment, while taking care of a toddler and helping a second grader with online school. Workplaces that are better able to provide equal opportunity for their employees to perform will make more equitable decisions when it comes to raises, bonuses, and promotion opportunities.

After the social justice protests of 2020, many employers made public statements of support for racial diversity. However, making necessary changes has proved more difficult[3]. For example, one research lab I am familiar with identified that its workforce was not diverse, despite the fact that it generally adhered to Whole-Person principles and created a welcoming organizational culture. After conversations, leaders there recognized that they generally recruited scientists from only a small handful of graduate programs where they had personal connections and had invested little in developing a more diverse talent pipeline. They are now making some long-overdue changes.

Further, there is no room for harassment at a Whole-Person Workplace. All employees should feel physically and psychologically safe at work, and free to be themselves. Everyone, but especially managers, need to be fully oriented on these issues, and employers should conduct thorough background checks during the hiring process. Claims of harassment need to be taken seriously, using proper grievance procedures and in-depth investigations. Whole-Person Workforces do not force arbitration and non-disclosure agreements that hide problems from public scrutiny[4]. Instead, they create inclusive cultures and enforce norms, even if doing so results in a short-term reputational hit. Whole Person Workplaces do not protect high-profile abusers over those they hurt.

Finally, there is considerable evidence that companies with more diverse leadership teams outperform those without[5]. This makes sense, as diversity helps companies appreciate and understand different perspectives, become more in tune with the changing needs of a diverse set of customers and stakeholders, and are better able to manage diverse workforces. But you can't reap the benefits of diversity if your culture, consciously or unconsciously, fails to properly value individual differences.

If you don't retain, invest in, and fully appreciate the contributions of the full range of whole people you employ, you fail to live up to Whole-Person Workplace values and, therefore, are less likely to thrive as a company.

ENDNOTES

PREFACE AND INTRODUCTION

1. The quotes and anecdotes throughout the book are primarily derived from my interviews, along with research and attributed quotes from other sources. I lightly edited quotes for readability and, sometimes, to take out identifying details.
2. https://www.youtube.com/watch?v=Jr8GK00mh-8
3. https://www.chieflearningofficer.com/2016/12/14/ryan-flipped-flex/
4. https://www.glassdoor.com/employers/blog/highest-rated-ceos-during-the-covid-19-crisis/
5. https://fortune.com/best-companies/2015/
6. https://www.linkedin.com/pulse/20130816200159-131079-employee-retention-now-a-big-issue-why-the-tide-has-turned/
7. The Whole-Person Workplace approaches of the following companies are included in this book: Adidas, ADP, Allagash Brewery, Allied Signal, Amazon, Applegate & Thorne-Thomsen, BASF, Best Buy, BirchBox, Boxed, Bristol-Myers Squibb, Cambia Health Solutions, Conagra Foods, Concord Management Services, Container Store, Convene, Costco, Deloitte, DePaul University, Dun & Bradstreet, EY, Flexjobs, GE, Gravity Payments, Hewlett-Packard Enterprises, Johnson & Johnson, Johnstone Supply, Jugtown Country Store, Merck, Microsoft, New Moon Natural Foods, Novartis, Olark, Ryan LLC, Salesforce, SAS, Shake Shack, Starbucks, The Gap, Trader Joe's, Uncommon Goods, Whole Foods, Zappos, and many more.
8. https://www.scottbehson.com/post/leading-by-example-ey-s-ceo-mark-weinberger-on-work-and-family

CHAPTER 1

1. https://www.flexjobs.com/guide-implementing-remote-work-success
2. https://www.bbc.com/worklife/article/20200514-how-the-post-pandemic-office-will-change
3. https://www.mckinsey.com/business-functions/operations/our-insights/managing-a-manufacturing-plant-through-the-coronavirus-crisis
4. https://www.bloomberg.com/news/articles/2020-10-20/are-offices-safe-during-covid-sensors-say-we-fail-to-socially-distance
5. https://www.mckinsey.com/business-functions/organization/our-insights/reimagining-the-office-and-work-life-after-covid-19
6. https://www.forbes.com/sites/williamarruda/2020/05/07/6-ways-covid-19-will-change-the-workplace-forever/#12d762af323e
7. http://workplacementalhealth.org/Employer-Resources/Working-Remotely-During-COVID-19
8. https://hbr.org/2020/09/4-strengths-of-family-friendly-work-cultures

CHAPTER 2

1. https://www.flexjobs.com/blog/post/flexjobs-gwa-report-remote-growth/
2. http://www.wmmsurveys.com/how_men_flex_report_wmri.html
3. https://www.forbes.com/sites/rachelsandler/2020/08/27/heres-when-major-companies-plan-to-go-back-to-the-office/#c08aa9d361c5
4. https://www.cnn.com/2020/05/22/tech/work-from-home-companies/index.html
5. https://www.wsj.com/articles/employees-feel-pressured-as-bosses-order-them-back-to-offices-during-pandemic-11594821600
6. Hall, D. T. (1990). Promoting work/family balance: An organization-change approach. Organizational Dynamics, 18(3), 5-18.
7. https://www.inc.com/justin-bariso/microsofts-new-6-word-remote-work-policy-is-brilliant-heres-why-your-company-should-steal-it.html
8. Behson, S.J. (2015). The Working Dad's Survival Guide: How to Succeed at Work and at Home. Motivational Press: Melbourne, Florida.
9. https://www.thebalancecareers.com/job-share-good-and-bad-1918169
10. https://www.shrm.org/hr-today/news/hr-news/Pages/xms_021497.aspx
11. https://hbr.org/2016/09/would-amazons-30-hour-week-experiment-work-in-your-company
12. https://www.instyle.com/lifestyle/working-moms-office-space-pandemic-hotel
13. http://blogs.hbr.org/2014/03/increase-workplace-flexibility-and-boost-performance/
14. https://time.com/2850144/white-house-working-dads/
15. https://hbr.org/2014/12/flex-time-doesnt-need-to-be-an-hr-policy
16. http://blogs.hbr.org/2014/03/increase-workplace-flexibility-and-boost-performance/
17. https://marginalrevolution.com/marginalrevolution/2014/01/claudia-goldin-on-the-gender-pay-gap.html
18. https://www.shrm.org/hr-today/news/hr-magazine/pages/0412quirk.aspx
19. https://www.scottbehson.com/post/my-5-favorite-parts-of-the-white-house-summit-on-working-families
20. https://nwlc.org/blog/tale-two-macys/
21. http://blogs.hbr.org/2014/03/googles-scientific-approach-to-work-life-balance-and-much-more/
22. https://www.flexjobs.com/guide-implementing-remote-work-success
23. https://www.scottbehson.com/post/negotiating-for-flexibility-at-work-why-bosses-say-no-to-flexible-work-arrangements-and-what-yo
24. https://hbr.org/2016/04/work-life-balance-is-easier-when-your-manager-knows-how-to-assess-performance
25. https://www.flexjobs.com/guide-implementing-remote-work-success

CHAPTER 3

1. https://www.nwlc.org/sites/default/files/pdfs/state_by_state_analysis.pdf
2. https://www.nationalpartnership.org/our-work/resources/economic-justice/paid-leave/paid-leave-good-for-business.pdf

3. https://hbr.org/2018/09/how-companies-can-ensure-maternity-leave-doesnt-hurt-womens-careers

4. Behson, S.J. (2015). The Working Dad's Survival Guide: How to Succeed at Work and at Home. Motivational Press: Melbourne, Florida.

5. Beacom, A., S.J. Behson, L. Hammer, and T. McDade. 2018. "Re-Conceiving Parental Leave as a Developmental Opportunity for New Parents, Work Teams, Managers and Organizations." Panel Symposium at the Work and Family Researchers Network Conference, June, Washington, D.C.

6. https://careers.microsoft.com/us/en/usbenefits

7. https://www.pewresearch.org/fact-tank/2019/12/16/u-s-lacks-mandated-paid-parental-leave/

8. https://www.unicef.org/media/55696/file/Family-friendly%20policies%20research%202019.pdf

9. https://www.pewresearch.org/fact-tank/2019/12/16/u-s-lacks-mandated-paid-parental-leave/

10. Brody, L. S. (2017). The Fifth Trimester: The Working Mom's Guide to Style, Sanity, and Success After Baby. Anchor.

11. https://www.worldatwork.org/docs/research-and-surveys/survey-report-survey-of-paid-parental-leave-in-the-us.pdf

12. https://www.dol.gov/agencies/whd/fmla/final-rule/

13. In order, California, New Jersey, Rhode Island, New York, Washington, Washington D.C., Massachusetts, Connecticut, and Oregon. https://www.ncsl.org/research/labor-and-employment/paid-family-leave-resources.aspx

14. https://www.fatherly.com/love-money/boxed-ceo-chieh-huang-paternity-leave-perks/

15. https://www.shrm.org/resourcesandtools/tools-and-samples/policies/pages/paid-parental-leave-policy.aspx

16. Behson, S.J. (2015). The Working Dad's Survival Guide: How to Succeed at Work and at Home. Motivational Press: Melbourne, Florida.

17. https://hrexecutive.com/heres-why-a-recent-settlement-may-help-new-dads/

18. https://www.eeoc.gov/laws/guidance/enforcement-guidance-pregnancy-discrimination-and-related-issues

19. Behson, S.J. (2019) Successfully Enrolling Men in Organizational Work-Family Programs. World at Work Journal, 28(1), 31-39.

20. https://hbr.org/2013/08/whats-a-working-dad-to-do

21. Friedman, R. (2014). The best place to work: The art and science of creating an extraordinary workplace. TarcherPerigee.

22. https://www.wsj.com/articles/the-bosses-who-walk-the-walk-on-paternity-leave-11558949400

23. https://www.acuitymag.com/people/baby-steps-for-working-mums-and-dads

24. https://www.benefitnews.com/news/salesforce-promotes-employee-on-maternity-leave

25. Uhereczky, Agnes & Vadkerti, Zoltán. (2018). One Life - how the most forward looking organisations leverage work-life integration to attract talent and foster employee wellbeing.

CHAPTER 4

1. Brody, L. S. (2017). The Fifth Trimester: The Working Mom's Guide to Style, Sanity, and Success After Baby. Anchor.
2. http://www.itsworkingproject.com/
3. http://www.pewsocialtrends.org/2013/03/14/modern-parenthood-roles-of-moms-and-dads-converge-as-they-balance-work-and-family/
4. https://thebenefitsguide.com/should-you-subsidize-child-care-for-your-employees/
5. https://gusto.com/blog/benefits/child-care-benefit
6. https://allthingstalent.org/2019/01/23/on-site-childcare-facility/
7. https://www.glassdoor.com/blog/companies-with-onsite-childcare/
8. https://www.shrm.org/resourcesandtools/hr-topics/employee-relations/pages/many-workplaces-consider-child-care-subsidies.aspx
9. Uhereczky, Agnes & Vadkerti, Zoltán. (2018). One Life - how the most forward looking organisations leverage work-life integration to attract talent and foster employee wellbeing.
10. https://www.brighthorizons.com/family-solutions/back-up-care
11. https://www.newyorkfamily.com/coworking-spaces-for-women-new-york/
12. https://www.bizjournals.com/portland/blog/techflash/2015/05/working-portland-mothers-could-get-a-shared-office.html
13. https://www.cdc.gov/media/releases/2016/p0822-breastfeeding-rates.html
14. https://www.cdc.gov/breastfeeding/data/facts.html#:~:text=3-,Why%20Do%20Mothers%20Stop%20Breastfeeding%20Early%3F,long%20as%20they%20intend%20to.
15. https://www.dol.gov/agencies/whd/nursing-mothers/faq
16. https://www.harpersbazaar.com/culture/features/a21203672/why-women-stop-breastfeeding-pumping-at-work/
17. https://hbr.org/2016/04/complying-with-family-friendly-leave-policies-is-not-enough
18. https://www.mindfulreturn.com/is-milk-stork-worth-it/
19. https://www.lamag.com/guide/shopping/pump-station/
20. https://www.forbes.com/sites/shelleyzalis/2019/02/22/the-motherhood-penalty-why-were-losing-our-best-talent-to-caregiving/
21. Uhereczky, Agnes & Vadkerti, Zoltán. (2018). One Life - how the most forward looking organisations leverage work-life integration to attract talent and foster employee wellbeing.
22. http://onlinelibrary.wiley.com/doi/10.1111/josi.2013.69.issue-2/issuetoc
23. http://onlinelibrary.wiley.com/doi/10.1111/josi.12016/abstract
24. http://onlinelibrary.wiley.com/doi/10.1111/josi.12018/abstract
25. http://onlinelibrary.wiley.com/doi/10.1111/josi.12017/abstract
26. http://onlinelibrary.wiley.com/doi/10.1111/josi.12015/abstract

CHAPTER 5

1. https://www2.deloitte.com/content/dam/Deloitte/global/Documents/About-Deloitte/gx-2018-millennial-survey-report.pdf

2. https://hbr.org/2018/03/employee-surveys-are-still-one-of-the-best-ways-to-measure-engagement

3. https://smallbusiness.chron.com/run-employee-engagement-focus-group-23869.html

4. https://www.insperity.com/blog/how-to-conduct-an-exit-interview-the-right-way/

5. Uhereczky, Agnes & Vadkerti, Zoltán. (2018). One Life - how the most forward looking organisations leverage work-life integration to attract talent and foster employee wellbeing.

6. https://www.intuitbenefits.com/life-stages/six-benefits-tips-by-age

7. https://www.glassdoor.com/employers/blog/5-job-benefits-attract-quality-candidates/

8. https://www.cnn.com/travel/article/unused-vacation-days-trnd/index.html

9. https://www.ey.com/en_us/careers/total-rewards

10. https://www.greatplacetowork.com/resources/blog/what-we-can-learn-from-eys-bold-people-practice

11. https://www.goingconcern.com/ey-flexible-vacation-policy-pto/

12. https://www.paycor.com/resource-center/state-paid-sick-leave-laws

13. https://www.nytimes.com/2020/02/11/parenting/sandwich-generation-costs.html

14. https://www.ey.com/en_us/careers/total-rewards

15. https://www.shrm.org/resourcesandtools/tools-and-samples/toolkits/pages/managingworklifefitdependentcare.aspx

16. https://www.workforce.com/news/the-benefits-of-offering-backup-elder-care-to-employees

17. https://www.businessnewsdaily.com/10007-encourage-employee-volunteer-work.html

18. https://www.shrm.org/resourcesandtools/tools-and-samples/hr-qa/pages/employersponsoredvolunteerism.aspx#:~:text=Many%20employers%20encourage%20employees%20to,paid%20time%20off%20for%20volunteering

19. https://www.charities.org/news/blog/7-outstanding-corporate-matching-gift-programs

20. https://www.zenefits.com/workest/6-example-vto-policies/

21. http://www.trueimpact.com/social-impact-resources/bid/68386/Measuring-Volunteerism-Impacts-on-Employee-Development

22. https://fortune.com/2018/02/09/best-workplaces-giving-back-2018/

23. https://www.glassdoor.com/blog/10-companies-with-unique-volunteer-opportunities/

24. https://careervision.org/lifelong-learning-lifelong-success/

25. https://www.forbes.com/sites/meghanbiro/2018/07/23/developing-your-employees-is-the-key-to-retention-here-are-4-smart-ways-to-start/#5d152ba83734

26. https://www.shrm.org/resourcesandtools/tools-and-samples/toolkits/pages/educationalassistanceprograms.aspx

27. https://www.edsurge.com/news/2019-07-25-5-years-since-starbucks-offered-

to-help-baristas-attend-college-how-many-have-graduated

28. https://www.forcebrands.com/blog/2018/10/03/global-food-beverage-companies-employee-retention/

29. https://www.aboutamazon.com/working-at-amazon/career-choice

30. https://www.linkedin.com/learning/

31. https://www.brewbound.com/news/allagash-brewing-introduces-saison/

32. Technically, there are several different types of retirement plans, including 403b's. I will use 401k as an overall term because it is the most common

33. https://www.irs.gov/retirement-plans/plan-sponsor/401k-plan-overview

34. https://www.investopedia.com/ask/answers/10/why-employer-matches-401k.asp

35. https://www.businessinsider.com/costco-jobs-best-part-2018-4#the-majority-of-workers-said-that-pay-benefits-and-job-security-are-a-huge-draw-1

36. https://www.forbes.com/sites/zackfriedman/2020/02/03/student-loan-debt-statistics/#6d66b32d281f

37. https://loans.usnews.com/articles/which-employers-offer-student-loan-repayment

38. https://www.fastcompany.com/90272438/help-paying-off-your-student-loans-is-a-great-perk-if-you-can-get-it

39. https://mywealthsolutions.com.au/blog/budgeting/forced-savings-plan/

40. https://www.insidehighered.com/quicktakes/2019/05/22/pwc-pays-25-million-employees-student-debt

41. https://www.fatherly.com/love-money/father-of-the-year-chieh-huang-boxed-parents/

42. https://www.savingforcollege.com/article/state-tax-incentives-for-employer-529-plan-matching

43. https://www.cnbc.com/2017/06/06/boxed-ceo-chieh-huang-offers-generous-employee-benefits-to-keep-talent.html

44. https://www.shrm.org/resourcesandtools/tools-and-samples/hr-qa/pages/crisisfundwhatisatax-advantagedemployeecrisisfund,andwhataretheguidelinesforestablishingsuchafund.aspx

45. https://www.shrm.org/resourcesandtools/hr-topics/benefits/pages/emergency-relief-funds-throw-employees-lifeline-during-pandemic.aspx

CHAPTER 6

1. https://www.brainyquote.com/authors/joyce-brothers-quotes

2. https://www.shrm.org/resourcesandtools/tools-and-samples/how-to-guides/pages/howtocreatealeavedonationprogram.aspx

3. https://www.youtube.com/watch?v=bsLTh9Gity4

4. https://www.youtube.com/watch?v=axlWBn7YQA4

5. https://www.inc.com/robert-glazer/5-lessons-herb-kelleher-of-southwest-airlines-taught-me-about-life-leadership.html

6. Dweck, C. S. (2008). Mindset: The new psychology of success. Random House Digital, Inc.

7. https://nothingventured.rocks/hire-people-with-a-growth-mindset-

b6554c0abe3

8. Goleman, D. (2006). Emotional intelligence. Bantam.

9. Lynn, A. (2008). The EQ interview: Finding employees with high emotional intelligence. Amacom.

10. https://positivepsychology.com/emotional-intelligence-interview-questions/

11. https://www.youtube.com/watch?v=bsLTh9Gity4

12. https://hbr.org/1995/03/the-ceo-as-coach-an-interview-with-alliedsignals-lawrence-a-bossidy

13. Friedman, R. (2014). The best place to work: The art and science of creating an extraordinary workplace. TarcherPerigee.

14. Buckingham, M., & Coffman, C. (2014). First, break all the rules: What the world's greatest managers do differently. Simon and Schuster.

15. http://blogs.hbr.org/2014/03/increase-workplace-flexibility-and-boost-performance/

16. https://www.statestreet.com/content/dam/statestreet/documents/about/Flex%2BOverview%2B2012.pdf

17. Richard, Hackman J., and Greg Oldham. "Motivation through the design of work: Test of a theory." Organizational behavior and human performance 16, no. 2 (1976): 250-279.

18. Behson, S. J., Eddy, E. R., & Lorenzet, S. J. (2000). The importance of the critical psychological states in the job characteristics model: A meta-analytic and structural equations modeling examination. Current research in social psychology, 5(12), 170-189.

19. Pink, D. H. (2011). Drive: The surprising truth about what motivates us. Penguin.

20. https://www.youtube.com/watch?v=u6XAPnuFjJc

21. https://knowledge.wharton.upenn.edu/article/putting-a-face-to-a-name-the-art-of-motivating-employees/

22. https://hbr.org/2013/10/dont-treat-your-career-marathon-like-a-sprint

23. Pfeffer, J. (2018). Dying for a paycheck: How modern management harms employee health and company performance—and what we can do about it. HarperCollins.

24. https://www.psychologytoday.com/us/blog/the-perfect-blend/201206/new-study-shows-we-are-overworked-and-overwhelmed

25. https://hbr.org/2015/07/just-because-youre-happy-doesnt-mean-youre-not-burned-out

26. https://hbr.org/2014/06/work-life-balance-through-interval-training

27. https://snacknation.com/blog/employee-wellness-program-ideas/

28. https://newatlas.com/right-to-disconnect-after-hours-work-emails/55879/

29. https://money.cnn.com/2017/01/02/technology/france-office-email-workers-law/

30. https://www.workforce.com/news/part-of-boston-consulting-groups-success-comes-from-looking-out-for-its-workers

31. https://worklifelaw.org/publications/Disruptive-Innovations-New-Models-of-Legal-Practice-webNEW.pdf

32. https://hbr.org/2013/10/dont-treat-your-career-marathon-like-a-sprint

CHAPTER 7

1. NYT https://www.nytimes.com/2015/04/14/business/owner-of-gravity-payments-a-credit-card-processor-is-setting-a-new-minimum-wage-70000-a-year.html
2. https://www.amazon.com/Worth-Million-Dollar-Minimum-Revealed-Business-ebook/dp/B081D667SW
3. https://money.cnn.com/interactive/technology/15-questions-with-dan-price/index.html
4. Maslow, A. H. (1943). A theory of human motivation. Psychological Review, 50(4), 370-96.
5. Pink, D. H. (2011). Drive: The surprising truth about what motivates us. Penguin.
6. https://www.fool.com/personal-finance/2019/11/02/5-quotes-that-will-make-you-rethink-your-personal.aspx
7. https://www.huffingtonpost.in/work-better-training/5-reasons-why-some-managers-dread-performance-appraisals_a_21719978/
8. https://hbr.org/2019/01/why-most-performance-evaluations-are-biased-and-how-to-fix-them
9. https://www.gallup.com/workplace/249332/harm-good-truth-performance-reviews.aspx
10. https://www.reviewsnap.com/blog/the-case-for-more-frequent-performance-reviews/
11. https://hbr.org/2020/06/how-to-do-performance-reviews-remotely
12. https://www.hrzone.com/community-voice/blogs/appraisly/performance-appraisal-forms-the-good-the-bad-and-the-ugly
13. https://www.managementstudyhq.com/advantages-and-disadvantages-of-mbo.html
14. https://www.shrm.org/resourcesandtools/hr-topics/employee-relations/pages/360degreeperformance.aspx
15. https://www2.deloitte.com/us/en/insights/focus/human-capital-trends/2017/redesigning-performance-management.html
16. https://hbr.org/2015/04/reinventing-performance-management
17. https://www.rebelplaybook.com/bonus-plays/ditching-performance-ratings-and-annual-reviews-gap
18. https://www.theatlantic.com/politics/archive/2015/08/how-millennials-forced-ge-to-scrap-performance-reviews/432585/
19. https://hbr.org/2016/04/work-life-balance-is-easier-when-your-manager-knows-how-to-assess-performance
20. https://www.youtube.com/watch?v=Jr8GK00mh-8
21. https://www.chieflearningofficer.com/2016/12/14/ryan-flipped-flex/
22. https://fortune.com/best-companies/2020/ryan/
23. https://hbr.org/2014/12/flex-time-doesnt-need-to-be-an-hr-policy
24. https://www.youtube.com/watch?v=bsLTh9Gity4

25. Lewis, L. (2005). The Trader Joe's adventure: turning a unique approach to business into a retail and cultural phenomenon. Kaplan Publishing.
26. https://money.com/what-its-like-to-work-at-trader-joes/
27. https://www.pymnts.com/news/retail/2018/whole-foods-amazon-acquisition-ecommerce-employees-union/
28. https://www.hrtechnologist.com/articles/hr-compliance/pay-transparency-hr-strategy/
29. https://www.youtube.com/watch?v=G4rDIrKUgyQ
30. http://standfor.containerstore.com/18-awesome-years-on-fortunes-100-best-list
31. https://www.indeed.com/cmp/Shake-Shack/salaries/Cashier https://fortune.com/2016/09/14/shake-shack-pay-rate/
32. https://www.businessinsider.com/costco-jobs-best-part-2018-4
33. https://www.cnbc.com/2020/09/25/jim-cramer-buy-costcos-stock-after-its-absurd-post-earnings-dip.html
34. https://bcorporation.net/about-b-corps
35. NYT https://www.nytimes.com/2015/04/14/business/owner-of-gravity-payments-a-credit-card-processor-is-setting-a-new-minimum-wage-70000-a-year.html
36. https://www.pnas.org/content/107/38/16489.full
37. https://twitter.com/DanPriceSeattle
38. https://www.nytimes.com/2019/03/30/opinion/sunday/dan-price-minimum-wage.html
39. https://www.inc.com/jessica-stillman/remember-that-company-with-70k-minimum-wage-heres-how-its-doing-now.html
40. https://komonews.com/news/local/baby-boom-seattle-company-70k-minimum-wage-caused-workforce-to-grow
41. https://www.washingtonpost.com/outlook/2020/08/12/employees-pay-cuts-productivity/
42. https://www.idahostatesman.com/news/business/article244968805.html

CHAPTER 8

1. https://www.hrdive.com/news/rethinking-employee-wellness-perks-in-the-age-of-the-coronavirus/583389/
2. https://hbr.org/2010/12/whats-the-hard-return-on-employee-wellness-programs
3. https://www.health.harvard.edu/blog/do-employee-wellness-programs-actually-work-2019081317503
4. https://www.shrm.org/resourcesandtools/tools-and-samples/how-to-guides/pages/howtoestablishanddesignawellnessprogram.aspx
5. https://hbr.org/2010/12/whats-the-hard-return-on-employee-wellness-programs
6. https://snacknation.com/blog/employee-wellness-program-ideas/
7. https://risepeople.com/blog/workplace-wellness-programs/
8. https://hbr.org/2017/01/workplace-wellness-programs-could-be-putting-your-health-data-at-risk

9. https://www.usatoday.com/story/money/careers/2018/07/10/ask-hr-company-health-risk-assessment-telecommute-work-home/763656002/
10. https://www.cnn.com/2015/09/28/health/workplace-wellness-privacy-risk-exclusive/index.html
11. https://risepeople.com/blog/workplace-wellness-programs/
12. https://www.inc.com/guides/2010/04/bike-to-work.html
13. https://www.shrm.org/resourcesandtools/hr-topics/benefits/pages/worksitecafeteria.aspx
14. https://www.cdc.gov/nccdphp/dnpa/pdf/Healthy_Worksite_Food.pdf
15. https://benefitsbridge.unitedconcordia.com/healthy-snacks-workplace-vending-machine/
16. https://www.fastcompany.com/3024747/5-reasons-to-never-eat-lunch-at-your-desk-again

17. Stringer, L. (2016). The Healthy Workplace: How to Improve the Well-Being of Your Employees---and Boost Your Company's Bottom Line. Amacom.
18. https://www.mayoclinic.org/healthy-lifestyle/adult-health/in-depth/office-ergonomics/art-20046169
19. https://www.shrm.org/resourcesandtools/hr-topics/risk-management/pages/prevent-sprains-strains-workplace.aspx
20. https://www.workingamerica.org/fixmyjob/workingconditions/physically-demanding-work
21. https://qz.com/983409/lowes-is-giving-its-workers-exoskeletons-to-help-lift-very-heavy-things/
22. https://www.workdesign.com/2020/01/how-a-healthy-workspace-can-transform-your-office-culture/
23. https://www.shrm.org/resourcesandtools/tools-and-samples/hr-qa/pages/whatisaneap.aspx
24. https://www.insperity.com/blog/employee-assistance-programs-a-powerful-employee-perk/
25. https://wellspringfs.org/coronavirus
26. https://www.sciencedirect.com/science/article/abs/pii/0091743588900692
27. Stringer, L. (2016). The Healthy Workplace: How to Improve the Well-Being of Your Employees---and Boost Your Company's Bottom Line. Amacom.
28. https://hbr.org/2010/12/whats-the-hard-return-on-employee-wellness-programs
29. https://www.transamericacenterforhealthstudies.org/docs/default-source/wellness-page/2018EmployerGuide.pdf?sfvrsn=4
30. https://hbr.org/2010/12/whats-the-hard-return-on-employee-wellness-programs
31. https://www.corporatewellnessmagazine.com/article/gamification-to-make-wellness-fun-and-engaging
32. https://www.shrm.org/resourcesandtools/hr-topics/benefits/pages/real-roi-wellness.aspx

CHAPTER 9

1. https://www.npr.org/2015/06/28/418147961/the-man-who-saved-southwest-airlines-with-a-10-minute-idea
2. https://portal.fdu.edu/newspubs/magazine/05ws/tribute.htm
3. Connors & Smith (2012). Change the Culture, Change the Game: The Breakthrough Strategy for Energizing Your Organization and Creating Accountability for Results. Portfolio.
4. https://www.shrm.org/resourcesandtools/tools-and-samples/toolkits/pages/understandinganddevelopingorganizationalculture.aspx
5. https://hbr.org/2002/07/make-your-values-mean-something
6. http://blogs.hbr.org/cs/2013/08/whats_a_working_dad_to_do.html
7. Behson, S.J. (2019) Successfully Enrolling Men in Organizational Work-Family Programs. World at Work Journal, 28(1), 31-39.
8. https://www.scottbehson.com/post/pioneering-fathers-needed-dare-to-be-visible-in-using-work-flexibility
9. https://www.businessinsider.com/zappos-head-of-hr-four-weeks-onboarding-hire-great-people-2019-11
10. https://www.fastcompany.com/3004953/how-sas-became-worlds-best-place-work
11. https://www.growthink.com/content/two-most-important-quotes-business
12. https://www.forbes.com/sites/lizryan/2014/02/10/if-you-cant-measure-it-you-cant-manage-it-is-bs/?sh=6efe363a7b8b
13. https://corpgov.law.harvard.edu/2019/02/06/the-wells-fargo-cross-selling-scandal-2/
14. https://www.forbes.com/sites/forbestechcouncil/2018/01/02/why-company-culture-needs-to-be-part-of-your-2018-budget/?sh=2b425e9b11f4
15. https://www.worldatwork.org/workspan/articles/how-organizations-are-handling-rewards-and-hazard-pay-decisions-in-a-covid-19-world
16. http://www.thestaffingstream.com/2018/06/07/why-you-should-give-your-company-culture-a-budget/
17. https://www.greatplacetowork.com/resources/blog/5-culture-lessons-from-100-best-company-salesforce
18. Hamper, B. (2008). Rivethead: Tales from the assembly line. Grand Central Publishing.
19. http://principlesofmanagement.org/blog/2012/11/22/tqm-in-gm/
20. https://www.thestreet.com/video/august-5-1983-att-split-into-eight-regional-companies
21. https://www.nytimes.com/2002/01/19/opinion/enron-s-vision-and-values-thing.html
22. https://hbr.org/2002/07/make-your-values-mean-something
23. https://genius.com/Peter-tosh-stand-firm-lyrics
24. https://www.basf.com/us/en/careers/why-join-basf/what-you-will-get.html

CHAPTER 10

1. https://www.chieflearningofficer.com/2016/12/14/ryan-flipped-flex/

2. https://www.forbes.com/sites/lisacurtis/2019/11/23/why-your-lack-of-diversity-is-hurting-your-business/?sh=65cee6172782
3. https://www.bcg.com/en-us/publications/2018/how-diverse-leadership-teams-boost-innovation
4. https://onlinelibrary.wiley.com/doi/abs/10.1111/1468-2338.00201
5. https://qz.com/work/1495333/1495333/
6. https://www.linkedin.com/pulse/20130816200159-131079-employee-retention-now-a-big-issue-why-the-tide-has-turned/
7. https://www.fastcompany.com/3004953/how-sas-became-worlds-best-place-work
8. https://www.youtube.com/watch?v=utMy2RiM9wA
9. https://fortune.com/best-companies/2019/sas-institute/
10. https://www.sas.com/content/dam/SAS/documents/corporate-collateral/brochures/en-csr-employees-culture-110855.pdf
11. https://bcorporation.net/
12. https://www.youtube.com/watch?v=Jr8GK00mh-8
13. https://www.scottbehson.com/post/leading-by-example-ey-s-ceo-mark-weinberger-on-work-and-family
14. Behson, S.J. (2002). Coping with Family to Work Conflict: The Role of Informal Work Accommodations to Family. Journal of Occupational Health Psychology, 7(4), 324-341.
15. https://hbr.org/2014/12/flex-time-doesnt-need-to-be-an-hr-policy
16. Behson, S.J. (2015). The Working Dad's Survival Guide: How to Succeed at Work and at Home. Motivational Press: Melbourne, Florida.
17. Behson, S.J. (2015). The Working Dad's Survival Guide: How to Succeed at Work and at Home. Motivational Press: Melbourne, Florida.
18. Hammer, L., Kossek, E., Yragui, N., Bodner, T., & Hanson, G. (2009). Development and Validation of a Multidimensional Measure of Family Supportive Supervisor Behaviors (FSSB). Journal of management. 35. 837-856. 10.1177/0149206308328510.
19. Crain, T. L., & Stevens, S. C. (2018). Family-supportive supervisor behaviors: A review and recommendations for research and practice. *Journal of Organizational Behavior, 39*(7), 869–888. https://doi.org/10.1002/job.2320
20. Ulrich, Dave. (1997), HR Champions: The next agenda for adding value and delivering results. Harvard Business School Press, Boston.
21. Kotter, J. P. (2012). Leading change. Harvard business press.
22. https://www.workhuman.com/resources/globoforce-blog/6-big-mergers-that-were-killed-by-culture-and-how-to-stop-it-from-killing-yours
23. https://www.chieflearningofficer.com/2016/12/14/ryan-flipped-flex/
24. https://www.gallup.com/workplace/236213/why-need-best-friends-work.aspx
25. Blumenthal, Noah (2012). Be the Hero: Three Powerful Ways to Overcome Challenges in Work and Life. Berret-Kohler.
26. Behson, S.J. (2015). The Working Dad's Survival Guide: How to Succeed at Work and at Home. Motivational Press: Melbourne, Florida.
27. https://www.topresume.com/career-advice/company-culture-job-match

AFTERWORD

1. https://www.shrm.org/resourcesandtools/hr-topics/pages/diversity-equity-and-inclusion.aspx
2. https://theconversation.com/remote-work-worsens-inequality-by-mostly-helping-high-income-earners-136160
3. https://www.technologyreview.com/2020/09/05/1008187/racial-injustice-statements-tech-companies-racism-racecraft-opinion/
4. https://www.americanbar.org/groups/dispute_resolution/publications/dispute_resolution_magazine/2019/winter-2019-me-too/non-disclosure-agreements-and-the-metoo-movement/
5. https://www.mckinsey.com/business-functions/organization/our-insights/delivering-through-diversity

ACKNOWLEDGEMENTS

N O BOOK IS A SOLO PROJECT. I have so many people to thank for helping **The Whole-Person Workplace** become a reality.

I'd like to thank the many experts, HR professionals, business leaders, and others I've interviewed for the book. While many of them are quoted directly throughout, there are others who wanted their contributions to remain anonymous, and others who helped me learn about various topics by providing background information.

With apologies for those I've missed and those who wish to remain unnamed, I'd like to thank: Doreen Anthony, Amy Beacom, Julia Beck, Dave Bolotsky, Tony Bridwell, Cynthia Calvert, Karen Cardona, Mika Cross, Danielle DeBoer, Jessica DeGroot, Dan Domenech, Delta Emerson, Lisa Evans, Chris Geschickter, Billy Griffin, Elizabeth Hall, Ginny Kissling, Bill Plastine, Tom Prendergast, Brie Reynolds, Corinne Rice, Beth Rivera, Robert Russo, John Sarno, Brigid Schulte, Vicki Shabo, Stephanie Smith, Lauren Smith Brody, Alyssa Westring, and Eric Williams. Further, Steve Bear, Kent Fairfield, Ron Friedman, Stewart Friedman, Brad Harrington, Kenneth Matos, Anthony Oland, Michael Rothman, G. Brint Ryan, Brigid Schulte, Sara Sutton, Scott Tannenbaum, and Bruce Tracey read and gave me feedback on the book and, in some cases, generously provided testimonials. Of course, countless people gave me help and encouragement along the way.

I'd like to thank my colleagues and students at the Silberman College of Business at Fairleigh Dickinson University. Thanks to you, I have a career that nourishes me as a whole person. You provide me with a career of purpose and impact, as well as a great team to work with. Particular thanks to Drs. Capuano, Small, Balthazard, Rosman, Almeida, Wischnevsky, Jones, Fairfield, Bear, Harmon, and Hansbrough for their friendship, support, and the sabbatical that helped make the book a reality. To my

FDU students who motivate me to keep learning and help me to see the work world (and the actual world) with younger, more optimistic eyes-you inspire me, and I hope that, in turn, I do a good job in getting you ready to step up as business leaders with Whole-Person Workplace values.

I'd like to thank Tony Ferraro, Teri Whitten, and the team at Authors Place Press, who supported the vision of this book from the beginning, and Ashley Bernardi for her promotional wizardry.

Also, a very special thanks to you for reading my book. I hope I have given you the advice and encouragement you need to create a Whole-Person Workplace at your organization. You can always contact me at ScottBehson.com.

Finally, I'd like to thank my family for their unconditional love and support and for helping me be a better person every day. Amy and Nick, you are my heart.

31.) Businesses must cater to all stakeholders:
Investors/Shareholders | Customers | Community
Environment / Earth / Employees

32.) Purpose of this book (pg. 191)

33.) The importance of leadership (Pg. 210)

34.) Challenge → balancing fairness and response to employees having personal life struggles. Pg. 215
Customization vs. standardization of policies.
solutions perceived as unfair.

ABOUT THE AUTHOR

Scott Behson, PhD, is a professor of management and Silberman Global Faculty Fellow at Fairleigh Dickinson University. He is a national expert in work and family issues and the author of *The Working Dad's Survival Guide: How to Succeed at Work and at Home*- the best-selling book of advice and encouragement for fathers trying to balance work and family- and *We Hate Team Projects! A Friendly, Useful Guide for College Project Teams*- in use in college classrooms everywhere, helping professors and college students enjoy and succeed in their team projects.

Scott is an accomplished professional speaker and consultant who provides talks, workshops, webinars, and keynote addresses for corporate clients, not-for-profit organizations, and major conferences. He provides insight and perspective on whole-person workplaces, employer support for working parents, work and fatherhood, and related topics for some of the world's leading companies. Scott was a featured speaker at the United Nations' International Day of the Family and the White House's Summit for Working Families. He is represented by the BrightSight Group.

He has published over 30 academic journal articles and book chapters, presented over 50 times at national and international conferences, and won eight awards for his teaching, research, and service to students. Scott has written for *Harvard Business Review, TIME, Fast Company, Success, The Washington Post* and *The Wall Street Journal.* He frequently appears in media, including CBS, MSNBC, NPR, Fox News, and Bloomberg Radio, as well as many business and parenting podcasts.

Scott lives with his family in Nyack, NY and is a graduate of Cornell University and SUNY Albany. Check out his weekly **Whole-Person Workplace Videos,** on YouTube and LinkedIn, and go to ScottBehson.com for more information on his writing, speaking, and consulting activities.

PRAISE FOR SCOTT BEHSON'S PREVIOUS BOOK, THE WORKING DAD'S SURVIVAL GUIDE

If you're like most dads, you're facing an impossible tug of war between work and home. My advice? Read this book. In this smart, charming, and actionable guide, Scott Behson offers a practical toolkit for thriving in both domains. You'll discover how to make family time more memorable, how to negotiate more flexibility with your boss, and why you should pack at least one stuffed animal on every business trip. Behson is the rare writer who can communicate everything you need to know, while making you feel like you're just chatting over a beer with a good friend at a barbeque.

—Ron Friedman, Ph.D., author of *The Best Place to Work: The Art and Science of Creating an Extraordinary Workplace*

Finally! This is the book dads juggling work and family have been waiting for.

—Brad Harrington, PhD, Executive Director of the Boston College Center for Work and Family

Behson sets out to do one simple – but not at all easy – thing; help men feel confident and successful in both their work life and family life. Using the perfect combination of exercises, stories, insights, and practical strategies he accomplishes that goal with flying colors. There's no magic pill that will make you the best dad you can be. But with commitment, hard work, and Scott's guidance, you're well on your way.

—Armin Brott, author of *The Expectant Father* and *The New Father: A Dad's Guide to the First Year*

Cheers to Scott Behson for providing the 21st century working dad a roadmap for career and parenting success!

—Matt Schneider and Lance Somerfeld,
Co-Founders, City Dads Group.

I'm so glad Scott wrote this book, because he not only clearly shows the conflicts faced by many working dads, but he also provides actionable advice that will help dads find better solutions at work and at home. Scott's experience, and positivity, are a welcomed relief!

—Sara Sutton, Founder & CEO of FlexJobs

I wish I had this book when I was taking heat in the corporate world for being an active parent. The suggestions and exercises would have made a big difference, to both support the choices I was making, and help me build a community of other working dads so I would not feel alone.

—Greg Marcus, PhD, author of *Busting Your Corporate Idol:
Self-Help for the Chronically Overworked*

You might be a new dad who is craving this information, or an experienced dad interested in making a change, either way, Scott's words of wisdom and friendly tone will help guide you to a solution that's just right for you.

—Jessica DeGroot, Founder and President, ThirdPath Institute

Being an equal partner and involved father leads to a more meaningful, balanced life. Scott Behson draws brilliantly from his life and research to provide the stories, tips, and tools we need to become the fathers we want to be.

—Jeremy Adam Smith, author *The Daddy Shift*

Notes

1. Reminder of Scott's advice to me when I was first starting at FDU → "if you want to be a successful professor show your students that you care about them."

2. In my day, working long hours - doing whatever it takes, was a way to advance, get ahead. (see pg. 21) In the end, results matter, but being perceived as "all in" was important.

3. How do you create culture in a Zoom world?

4. The need for human interaction to foster culture. Note: similar to a professor teaching a class.

5. The value of experience (pgs 23-24) Do companies value experience?

6. Workload - the impact of streamlining.

7. Mergers, acquisitions, "right-sizing"

8. Job design

9. Technology brought "24/7" availability (↳ see pg. 112 + 114)

{ How ironic that we now see it as a solution

10. Can you work as hard - home vs. office. No distractions.

11. No office - loss of spontaneity. } "Manage by walking around"

12. Note: commute vs. office (bigger problem)

13. Remote (+) and Remote (-) see pg. 46/62

14. Research Yahoo work at home.

CPSIA information can be obtained at www.ICGtesting.com
Printed in the USA
LVHW080727100821
694871LV00005B/142

9 781628 658156